FOUR DAYS AND FIVE NIGHTS

Corruptible Earth?
Incorruptible Crown!

KAY BRONSON

WESTBOW
PRESS®
A DIVISION OF THOMAS NELSON
& ZONDERVAN

Scripture quotations taken from the New American Standard Bible®,
Copyright © 1960, 1962, 1963, 1968, 1971, 1972, 1973, 1975, 1977, 1995
by The Lockman Foundation. Used by permission. (www.Lockman.org)

WestBow Press books may be ordered through
booksellers or by contacting:

WestBow Press
A Division of Thomas Nelson & Zondervan
1663 Liberty Drive
Bloomington, IN 47403
www.westbowpress.com
1 (866) 928-1240

ISBN: 978-1-5127-0756-4 (sc)
ISBN: 978-1-5127-0757-1 (e)

Library of Congress Control Number: 2015912755

Print information available on the last page.

WestBow Press rev. date: 08/20/2015

Dedicated to my loving and devoted parents,
Richard and Margie Bronson,
whom at this point in time have
gone to their rewards.

A NOTE FROM THE AUTHOR ...

Modern day technology and new advancements in science haven't only benefited the average person, as well as the professional work place, but I believe this testimony will also bring to light the opening of prison doors for hundreds of thousands severely handicapped children and adults, as well as myself, who through the invention of electronic devices have found a new way of self expression which wasn't otherwise possible. Several years ago, I was viewing a telecast of computer science. They showed a nine year old child with Cerebral Palsy who had never been able to talk. For the very first time she was able to punch out on the computer keyboard, "Mommy, I love you." In this introduction, I wish to make special acknowledgement of the Mooney family who provided a Brother Word Processor to make the completion of this story possible.

That this testimonial writing has develop into a book, to God be the glory. Without the inspiration of God's Holy Spirit, not one word of it could of or would if be written. Thanks also to my precious parents who have faithfully brought me up in the Lord from day one even until now. Without their spiritual encouragement and physical training, this writing wouldn't be possible. To this they would also say, "To God be the glory". They have even shared in some of the details of this piece. Ps. 115:1 "Not to us O Lord, but to Thy Name give Glory."

Also, I would like to give special acknowledgement to Cerebral Palsy people everywhere who have found in the Lord Jesus a real purpose for living in this life and rest in the blessed hope of their glorified bodies in heaven. Thus, the sub title CORRUPTIBLE EARTH? INCORRUPTIBLE CROWN. The thought in mind is that our precious Lord Jesus was willing to leave His INCORRUPTIBLE CROWN of glory to come into this CORRUPTIBLE EARTH so we, by His grace, might someday leave this CORRUPTIBLE EARTH to receive an INCORRUPTIBLE CROWN.

"In the future there is laid up for me the crown of righteousness, which the Lord, the righteous Judge will award to me, on that day; and not only to me, but also to all who have loved His appearing." The part of this verse which is special to me is "…not only to me, but also to all who love His appearing." 2 Tim. 4:8

Because of my parents being missionaries, I've had the privilege of learning to know and love peoples of other cultures who will by His Grace also love His appearing. This testimony is lovingly dedicated to them. It's my prayer this little piece of history will truly be His Story.

Words cannot express my deep gratitude for all the support and hard work my cousins, Harry Lane and Margaret Miller have provided over the past couple of years to bring this project to completion. To tell my story in my own words has been a deep longing in my heart for many years but I had reached a standstill until these precious friends stepped up and offered their assistance to help me make it a reality. We all hope this written testimony, with God's help, will bless and encourage all those who read it. I truly believe God has a plan for all our lives especially that we all come to know Him as our personal Savior. Thanks also to all my cousins for being so supportive throughout my life.

By Katherine L. Bronson

PROLOGUE

THANKS, PRAISE, LOVE AND GLORY
BE UNTO THEE ALMIGHTY GOD...
...Who Lives Forever and Ever, Amen.

Some people are Swedish, some people are German, and some people are Hispanic and so on. If anyone were to ask me what nationality I am, I would probably exclaim with a twinkle in my eye, "I'm Cerebral Palsy." We as Christians know, the joy of the Lord is our strength. Isaiah 40:31 (NASB), says, "They will mount up with wings like eagles, they will run and not get tired, they will walk and not become weary." I also believe a good sense of humor can be like a gift from the Lord.

One day, I was drying dishes for my mother. It's a good thing the glasses were plastic. Without warning, I had a muscle spasm in my hands, the glass shot like a bullet, straight up into the air, clearing my head. It flew across the room, we have a large kitchen, bounced off the kitchen door and came catapulting almost back to me, again. If I had been quick enough, in my reflexes, I'm sure I could have caught it on the way back. My reaction was the temptation to feel sorry for myself but when I realized what had happened, I was able to see the humor in it. Perhaps the glass being plastic helped me to see the humor. I thought to myself, 'Maybe Tommy Lasorda could use me on his baseball team as a pitcher.'

Sometimes my handicap can be to my own advantage. I can get other people to work for me. For instance, dining out at a cafeteria, someone else must carry my food tray. If I were to carry my own tray, first of all, the apple pie would be in the mashed potatoes and the iced tea would be in the roast beef by the time I got to the table and tray would be empty with a trail of food following behind me. The point I'm trying to make is, when we know the Lord Jesus Christ as our own personal Lord and Savior, He puts the right attitude in our hearts; therefore, this CORRUPTIBLE EARTH becomes a much better place to live. In the beginning God created this world perfect, but because of our sin and disobedience to God, there will always be suffering. I truly believe, although we have seen our Lord's healing touch in my physical progress, my greatest healing has been a spiritual one.

ONWARD

Thanksgiving 1988, found my parents and I seated in the worship center of the First Evangelical Free Church of Fullerton. It was a special time of reflection and thanksgiving for me. The following January, I would be celebrating my fiftieth birthday. I realize that most ladies would rather not tell their age, however, in my case it seems well and fitting that I should tell my age because of how abundantly good, merciful, and gracious our Lord has been to me. The first two years of my life were difficult. Doctors told my parents if I lived to be thirty years old, it would be a miracle. The apostle Paul said in Phil. 1:21 (NASB), "For to me, to live is Christ, and to die is gain." If I were to have died at thirty years old, it would have been gain for me. 2 Cor. 12:9 (NASB) "My grace is sufficient for you, for power is perfected in weakness." The desire of my heart is that the power of Christ be perfected through my weakness.

Due to the brain injury at birth, even my ability to simulate nourishment and hold it down was out of control. Several times my parents thought I wouldn't live. Parents feel helpless in a situation like this, not knowing what to do, but my parents knew how to pray and the Lord undertook for me in a very special way. We all have heard people say, "God helps those who help themselves." I believe God helps those who can't help themselves. He's able to do this because He is the true and living God. What we would call a miracle, to our wonderful God is a very simple task. Besides my inability to hold down nourishment, my immune system was very low. After returning home to the United States from Eastern Europe, where my parents were missionaries and where I was born, we were living in Chicago where the mission had its headquarters. As most people know, Chicago has a very severe climate. One day, mother happened to mention to the doctor that her home and family were in Southern California. The Lord is so faithful to His children when our lives are committed to Him. This doctor was one of the foremost top specialists in the country on Cerebral Palsy children. He told mother Southern California would be the best place for me to live. I would have a better chance of growing up out there. This was a very difficult decision for my parents to make. It meant they would need to leave the mission they were presently with. However, it seems when the Lord closes one door of opportunity, He opens another one, sometimes even better than before. Even preachers and missionaries sometimes have handicapped children but our wonderful Lord can work things out in such a way so that a handicapped child becomes a blessing to the ministry instead of a hindrance. Rev. 3:8 (NASB) " I know your deeds. Behold, I have put before you an open door which no one can shut, because you have a little power, and have kept My word, and have not denied My name." Not only were we on our way out to sunny California, they also found a way to curdle my milk

2

so I could hold it down. The substance used was called Lactic acid. Gradually I learned to eat normally. Now eating is one the things I do best.

"Don't crawl. You can walk." These were words of admonishment given to me one day by my mother that would someday cramp my style. My crawling days lasted a lot longer than most children. It got to the point where I could go almost as fast down on the floor as the other kids could go on their two feet. If my cousins, Margaret and Harry, wanted to get away from me, they would have to run. However, the time came to "put away childish things" 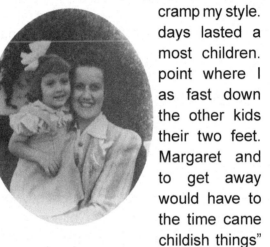 as they say, and get down to the serious business of learning to walk. Taking my first steps would be no time at all compared to a life time of learning to walk. My health was improving day by day in the warmth of the Southern California sunshine. Daddy had to take a secular job in an aircraft plant not too far away from where we lived, but the heart of my parents was still in the missions work. Their hearts still burned for the Christian brethren in Eastern Europe who were suffering cold and starvation cruelties of war. Although I was so very young, I still remember seeing our kitchen stacked very high, from the floor to the ceiling, with boxes of clothing and food to be shipped over to Eastern Europe. I was too young to understand about war, but I did know all those boxes stacked so very high were going to make some cold and hungry people very happy. It was during this time mother determined in her heart and mind that I was going to walk if it was the last thing she and I did together.

One thing which made it easier for my dad to work at Douglas Aircraft was his fond love for airplanes. We would be at the breakfast table and dad would exclaim, "There goes a DC6," or, "There goes a Piper Cab Comanche," before taking another bite from a second piece of toast. It always amazed me how my dad could know the make of an airplane going over head just by the sound of it.

Previous to mother's journey abroad, at the invitation of my dad to please come and be his wife, mother worked for several years in the department stores of Los Angeles to put herself through Bible College. It was during this time she learned the value of organizing her time and setting goals. This was to someday benefit her in being the wife of a missionary as well as raising a physically handicapped child. Besides the exhaustive daily routine of giving me physical and speech therapy, mother was a spotless housekeeper and excellent cook. A well balanced diet was also in order as part of my development. Frequently our home was open to preachers and missionaries passing through the area. Mother began each day with her devotional time with the Lord. This is when Isaiah 40:31 took on a realistic meaning for her. "Yet those who wait for the Lord will gain new strength; they will mount up with wings like eagles, they will run and not get tired, they will walk and not become weary." (NASB) Through my young and now more mature adult life, this daily quiet time with the Lord has been like a fortress for me in my own personal life.

First thing in the morning, I would be taken outdoors for what we called a sunbath. If used in moderation, the sun can be beneficial not only for Vitamin D, but to relax muscles. Next I would be brought back into the house, given a bath with water instead of the sun, hair washed and by this time things were in order, for exercises to begin. Each part of my body had to be manipulated from the head and neck to arms, hands and fingers, to legs, feet and toes. The new modern term for this is patterning; creating new patterns in the brain where the original ones were cut off. This actually is what mother did for me, day after day, except Saturdays and Sundays when we would rest. I can still remember mother tying a dish towel around my waist and we would go walking up and down the sidewalk in front of our apartment. This was the fun part. With mother's firm control of the dish towel, I could pretend I was walking alone. I could climb up and down steps with the security of mom holding firmly to the towel. This made me feel like a big kid. It seems there should be a spiritual application here somewhere. When our heavenly Father is holding us securely in His hands, we can rest in the knowledge that our spiritual walk will turn out all right. John 10:28 (NASB), "I give eternal life to them, and they shall never perish; and no one shall snatch them out of my Father's hand."

One evening, as we were seated at the dinner table, it seemed mother and daddy were in deep conversation. As usual, they would talk about the ministry, things going on at church or just dad's day at work. However, this time seemed to be different. I was still much too young to be concerned with adult communication. After eating the evening meal and dishes were stacked in the kitchen sink to be washed, I noticed dad was rolling up the rugs in the dining room, hallway and the one bedroom. Almost before my childish mind could realize what was happening, I was being kissed good night and tucked away in bed, in the next apartment across the yard. In those days, we still had so few worldly possessions it was possible to move from one apartment to another and be settled in just one short evening. The apartment we moved to was a less expensive one and lower on the ground. After all the excitement of moving and cleaning up another abode, it was time to get back to the more serious business of daily physical exercises and learning to walk. I was three or four years old and before anyone could blink an eye, it would be time to start kindergarten.

Mother would stand me up against a wall then start counting one, two, and three. When I'd start to fall forward against her hand, she'd push me up against the wall again. The counting would then start all over again. One, two, three, four – progress. One, two, three, four, five, "Kay, you might be ready for kindergarten after all," mom would say with a lilt in her voice which made me know she was happy. Perhaps mother was whispering a prayer. Sometimes all we need to ask of the Lord is HELP. A friend of ours whom we called Uncle Cecil, a carpenter, made a walker for me. It was constructed in such a way that I could crawl into it from the sides, up through the middle and out the top. It was painted blue. I often wondered why he didn't paint it pink for a little girl. Come to think of it, now, who in this world would feel any inspiration at all to paint something pink for a "tomboy", and a "tomboy" which is exactly what I was. While other little girls were wearing sweet little pink dresses and playing with dolls, I was wearing boy's blue jeans, cowboy boots and playing with a cap gun. I also had a basketball to bounce around and scramble after, just in case I got tired of chasing cowboys and Indians. I would listen to the Lone Ranger on the radio.

I never liked the walker too well, and to be honest about it, I could go faster by crawling. My tricycle was a great blessing to me. It gave my legs, arms and hands wonderful exercise. The seat had a back rest and pedal straps to hold my feet in place.

One Sunday after church, we were either at my aunt and uncle's house, or they were at our apartment. I don't remember which it was at this time, but my Uncle Harry propositioned me. "Kay", he said, "if you'll take just one step, I'll let you punch me in the chin." Well, I wasn't too concerned at that age about taking my first steps, but I did want to punch my Uncle in the chin. One reason why I walk as well as I do is because I did punch my Uncle in the nose. Although I was then more or less on my own two feet, if I got in a hurry, I would sometimes resort back to crawling again. This is when mother needed to get tough with me and say, "Katherine, don't crawl, you can walk." When mother called me Katherine instead of Kay, I knew she was dead serous. If she called me Katherine Lucille Bronson, then I knew for sure I was in deep trouble. One time I said, "Daddy, Katherine must be a swear word because every time mama calls me Katherine is when

7

she's mad at me." Even now, sometimes when I get in a hurry or exhausted, I wish I could crawl again or else fly.

It's everything in between that gives me trouble, or so it seems, but I know the Lord wants me to be thankful for the difficulties in life, at least this has been true with me. No matter what our own personal struggles might be, it seems we can all be thankful for what God has given to us.

There's a little song I learned in school. It's called:

Aren't You Glad You're You?

"Each morn, aren't you
glad you were born.
Think what you've got, the
whole day through."

By Bing Crosby

The spiritual counterpart to this, to me it seems, should be the famous old hymn:

Great is thy Faithfulness

"All I have needed Thy hand hath provided,
Great is thy faithfulness Lord unto me."

By Thomas O. Chisholm

KINDERGARTEN

The Inglewood Elementary School accepted me into their kindergarten even though, at that time, I was still considered very severely handicapped. The principal of the school had been my mother's teacher at one time. She was so 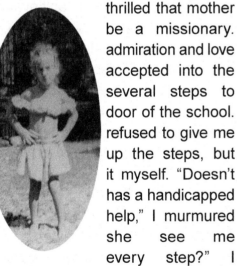 thrilled that mother had gone on to be a missionary. Because of her admiration and love for mother, I was accepted into the school. There were several steps to climb up to the front door of the school. Mother completely refused to give me any help at all going up the steps, but insisted that I do it myself. "Doesn't she realize she has a handicapped child and I need help," I murmured to myself. "Doesn't she see me struggling with every step?" I grumbled. "Doesn't she have any heart?" I continued as I saw her out of the corner of my eye, just standing there in case she would need to catch me in a fall. Now that I'm adult and more mature in my thinking, I realize the courage and self-control it must have taken for mother to

9

stand back and allow me to do it myself. Just like a young tree that must be allowed to blow in the wind in order to gain strength and stability, this is what mother was doing for me.

Because of mother's Bible college training, she could have left me many times to pursue her own ministry, but instead, in obedience to the Lord's will, she stayed home and worked to give me the best chance possible in life. Even so called "normal children" deserve the right to be given the best advantage in life. There's no greater gift that Christian parents can give back to the Lord than the precious souls of their own children.

To be honest about it, I can't ever remember the children in Kindergarten ever making fun of me. Perhaps they were still too young to realize I was a little different than they were. I do remember how they would run into me and push me down on the playground. Finally, it was decided that I would have to sit with the teacher during recess time. I loved my teacher very much and considered myself the luckier one to be given the privilege to sit with her.

Because of my being physically handicapped, most of my life has been with adults or older people. Situations and conditions of life have just forced it to be that way.

FAMILY ... AND
GRANDPA WATKINS

My Grandpa Watkins was a real blessing to me. After raising twelve children and thirty-five years of marriage, grandpa and grandma decided to separate and get a divorce. One day as I got older, perhaps thirteen or fourteen, grandma sat with me on the living room couch of her apartment and told me with tears in her eyes that she still really did love grandpa but it was just impossible for them to live together. If grandma made a move to another town, grandpa would move, too. They always lived within a few miles of each other. It got to be a family joke, that although grandma and grandpa couldn't live together, they really couldn't live without each other either. When grandpa died, the family discovered not only did grandpa buy his own burial plot with his small pension from the railroad, but had made arrangements and paid for grandma to be buried right on top of him. There was still enough money left in savings for each of the then eleven children still living to receive $35 each.

Grandpa rented a room where he could park his hat, as they say, but most of the time he would take turns staying with two or three of his married daughters. It was always a delight to me when it was our turn to have grandpa come and stay with us. I felt a real need for my grandpa during those early years. Now that I'm older, I realize just how much my grandfather needed me.

The school year was over, I completed kindergarten and I was no longer a baby. I was a little girl going into first grade. The principal of the school told mother she would insist on keeping me in the school if she was going to stay there, but as it was she would be retired. It was decided best for me to be sent to a special school in Los Angeles for physically handicapped children. Special, it really was, in more ways than one. There was only one problem. I was still only five years old and wouldn't be accepted into Washington Blvd. School until I was six. That would be the last part of January. I found myself counting away the months then the weeks, then the days and finally the hours. Mother and Dad always made sure my summer vacations were very enjoyable, so summer went by very fast.

We lived just a few miles from Grandma Watkins's house. I still remember three or four of my aunts and uncles were still home with grandma before getting married. We would sometimes all pile into the car and go down to Cabrillo Beach. I remember one time very vividly. I was seated on my Aunt Gloria's lap; everyone talking at the same time, trying to be heard one above the other one. My Uncle Billy, thirteen or fourteen at the time, was hanging his body half way out the window. Before arriving at the beach, we drove into a gas station. I noticed the man attending it was a white haired old man with a half bald head. For some strange reason, I felt my heart going out to him. I didn't really understand why Aunt Gloria gave me a little poke in the ribs, pointing out the window. She said, "Kay look, that's your grandpa." I already knew I loved him but now I understood why. After the car was all taken care of, we took off as if it were in a cloud of dust. I just couldn't take my eyes off grandpa. Out the back window, I kept my eyes focused on him until he was completely out of sight. Down at the beach, the family was having the time of their lives but I was still concerned about grandpa. It just didn't seem right to me that an old man like him would have to work so hard in a dirty old gas station. I wanted him to be with us. The Lord must have heard the heart cry of a very little girl because very soon after that, grandpa did quit his job.

Many times, when grandpa would come to stay with us, I would be sick with a very severe chest cold that would keep me in bed for two weeks or more at one time. Living near the ocean as we did, Inglewood was very cold and damp in winter. I was absent much from school because of it. "All she needs is an enema, grandpa would shout." Mother was hoping the neighbors wouldn't hear. Of course, grandpa would administer the enema himself. After raising twelve of his own children, what was one more little bare bottom to grandpa? After all that was taken care of, I would then be carried back to bed or if I wasn't too sick, I would be put on the living room couch. Grandpa would be seated beside me in his favorite armchair with a newspaper and his Villies cigars that I loved to smell. It was always a comfort to have grandpa with me.

One of my favorite things to do was to sit on the bathroom toilet seat and watch my daddy shave. It got to where I thought I could almost shave myself. One day, dad mistakenly left his razor out on the bathroom bowl. I stood and looked at that thing for the longest time then made a wrong decision. The desire was just more than I could contain. My parents knew beyond a shadow of any doubt that I was a full blooded tomboy, but they had no idea I would go so far as to try and shave my chin. When I realized I had cut myself, I thought sure I'd be in deep trouble with mom, but instead, she thought it to be so funny she took me over to show the next door neighbor lady. Since being grown up, I've been so grateful the Lord created me to be a girl. It's hard for me to understand why any woman would wish to trade places with a man. Our Lord had a terrific idea when he distinguished the species so why try to change it? We couldn't even if we wanted to. I still love to have a man open the door for me.

Finally, the great day came when I would board the school bus to go traveling into Los Angeles. The bus route was a two hour trip to and from school every day. Children are so resilient to every situation, it wasn't until I got older and began to rationalize that the long bus rides began to irritate me.

My kindergarten teacher had called on the phone to say good-bye. Just as you would suppose, mother completely refused to help me onto the school bus. By this time, the strength gained in my wobbly legs gave me more of a feeling of independence, or at least I wasn't irritated at mother for putting me on my own, the way she did at kindergarten. If mother hadn't been strong to put me on my own, I never would have been ready for Washington Boulevard.

The first day of school everyone is to tell where they live, give their name and answer the most important question of all, "Why do you have to come to this school?" Some kids said that they had Polio, then there were many different types of Cerebral Palsy. One little boy had such a severe heart condition he was in a wheelchair.

Mother always sent me off to school with my dresses starched and my hair looking absolutely perfect. By the time I got on the school bus in the late afternoon, my hair would be falling half into my eyes and my wrinkled up dress sometimes gave some clue as to what I had for lunch. If I lost a button off any part of my clothing, for some strange reason, I was always able to save it and bring it home to mamma, which only goes to show there must be some saving virtue in even the very least of us.

One day, I came home from school crying that I'll never be able to learn my ABC's. My lower lip was quivering, "It's just too hard." Mother, in her tender way, took me in her arms. "Honey", she said, "Don't worry, everything will come together in its own good time." Now as I sit here in front of my electric typewriter, I realize good old mom was right. **"But do not let this one fact escape your notice, beloved, that with the Lord one day is as a thousand years and a thousand years as one day." 2 Peter 3.8**

15

It really is funny how a simple thing like ABC's can seem to be a mountain to a little kid. You would have thought I had begun my first year of college instead of just the first grade. Although I haven't received any graduation diploma as such, gradually the Lord has enabled me to pick up as much knowledge as a person like me would ever need. For this, we praise the Lord.

Temporarily, mother had a breathing spell from giving me physical therapy and speech training. I was getting this at school; physical therapy (PT) three times a week, occupational therapy (OT) every day, and speech training once a week. Although this was necessary, still it took me away from classroom studies. It was during this time that mother took on the challenge to teach a Sunday school class of about thirty teenage girls. Many of them were new converts from non-Christian homes. Mother would sometimes have prayer meetings for them in the living room of our apartment. It made a lasting impression on my young mind to listen to teenage girls pray in the next room after I had already gone to bed. During the summer, Mother would take her Sunday school girls to the beach. I got to go too.

The winter of 1946 was another difficult one for me. I had the whooping cough. One month in bed also meant a whole month out of school. The doctor said I could die but if I pulled through this illness, without any doubt, I could live to a ripe old age. Coming home from work one day, daddy found mother crying in the kitchen. "Richard," mom said, "I don't think Kay is going to live." On that note daddy came quickly in to see how I was doing. "Daddy," I said, "mamma is a big baby." Both my parents gave a sigh of relief in the knowledge that I was still my ole' self and would certainly be all right.

Report card time came and I didn't pass. With a certain amount of severe colds and having whooping cough, I was out of school more than in school. Being taken out of classroom studies everyday or so for therapy certainly didn't help matters, either.

The therapist reassured my parents that if we developed my muscles while I was still very young before they set, my education could always come later. It was a real blow to me that I would have to stay another year in first grade. Our teacher gave me a whimsical smile and said, "Kay, the only reason why you want to pass into second grade is because Leddie is going into second grade." Leddie had Cerebral Palsy and was able to walk like me. The teacher knew Leddie and I were pals. Even with the disappointment of having to do the first grade over again, there were other signs of physical improvement. The straps were taken off the pedals of my tricycle. The little blue walker, acknowledged, I never really liked, was donated to the PT department at school.

Somehow mother found out Dr. Pearlstein from Chicago would be in Southern California lecturing at one of the largest hotels in Los Angeles. Dr. Pearlstein was the one who helped my parents so much with me when they were almost at wits end not knowing just what to do. Mother got the bright idea to dress me up in my Sunday best and we would go down to the Statler Hotel in hopes we might be able to see Dr. Pearlstein. He had so many other children he had helped just like me, it was doubtful he would even remember us, but it was worth a try.

When we got to the hotel it was wall to wall people. Everyone from the medical profession was there. Mother and I felt like intruders; of course, that's exactly what we were. We waited for hours, so it seemed, in the hotel lobby until the lecturing was over. At long last, the conference room doors burst open, a flood of people stormed out. Mother and I intruded ourselves into a long line to shake hands with Dr. Pearlstein. At times like this, mother would pick me up and carry me as my strength would give out shortly. Even to this very day, it's easier for me to walk a long way than to stand for even a short time. When we finally got up to where the doctor was, he thought a long time before realizing who we were. Then he said, "Mrs. Bronson, I wish all my mothers were as diligent about the rehabilitation of their handicapped children as you are." Mother was able to give a witness for the Lord instead of taking all the credit herself. Some mothers of handicapped children are victims of circumstances. A severely handicapped child may be born into an already large family. It's next to impossible to devote the necessary time for the betterment of the handicapped one. Because of my being physically handicapped, mother has been able to help and encourage other mothers of handicapped children who were almost at the breaking point. 2 Cor. 1:3,4 (NASB), "Blessed be the God and Father of our Lord Jesus Christ, the Father of mercies and God of all comfort; who comforts us in all our affliction so that we may be able to comfort those who are in any affliction with the comfort with which we ourselves are comforted by God." CORRUPTIBLE EARTH, INCORRUPTIBLE CROWN.

Although the winter of 1946 was a very difficult one for me, as I've already explained, the summer of that same year was a very special one for me. Our church was having two weeks of summer Daily Vacation Bible School. My physical therapist called mother and I back into school in order to instruct mother in how to continue my therapy at home during the summer months. The school hallways were deserted now but in my imagination the walls were still echoing the voices of many friends. Going to D.V.B.S. was a real change for me from the regular routine of daily exercises. I really enjoyed being with the normal children. On the last day of summer D.V.B.S., there was an assembly called for all the departments for a child evangelism meeting. I remember as if it were yesterday. The evangelist had a black handkerchief representing our hearts all dirty and black with sin, a red handkerchief representing Jesus' precious blood that He shed on the cross for our redemption and salvation. As I sat there down in the front of the church sanctuary, I knew my heart was as black as that black handkerchief with sin. It was my sin that made our dear Lord Jesus suffer more than anyone ever before him. Rom. 3:23, "For all have sinned and fall short of the glory of God." I knew this meant me. Rom. 6:23, "For the wages of sin is death, but the free gift of God is eternal life in Christ Jesus." I our Lord." (NASB) There was heavy conviction and a strong desire for repentance in my heart. The evangelist also showed us a white handkerchief. If we confess our sin, that we have no righteousness of our own, Jesus comes into our heart and makes it all clean and white, just as white as that white handkerchief. I could hardly wait for the invitation to be given. The Holy Spirit was working in my heart in a very definite way. As soon as the invitation was given, I ran down to the altar just as fast as a Cerebral Palsy girl could run. The evangelist's wife came down to the altar to pray with me. She knew my parents, she knew I was from a Christian home. She said, "Kay, just talk to the Lord, like you do at home." So I did. I said:

NOW I LAY ME DOWN TO SLEEP

"Now I lay me down to sleep,
I pray my soul to keep.
If I should die before I wake, I pray
the Lord my soul to take."

Author unknown

This is a famous child's bedtime prayer. It certainly isn't your traditional repentance prayer, but the Lord knew the sincerity of my heart and I was born again. There's a little song we would sing in Sunday school.

INTO MY HEART

"Into my heart, come Lord Jesus.
Come in today, come in to stay."

By Harry D. Clarke

"Verily I say unto you, whosoever shall not receive the Kingdom of God as a little child shall not enter it at all."

Luke 18:16-17, "Suffer the little children to come unto me, and forbid them not: for of such is the kingdom of God." It's so easy for a small child to come to the Lord Jesus. We as adults many times build up walls of unbelief that are so difficult to break down or tunnel through. Not only was I walking on my own two feet but now I was beginning my walk with the Lord. Now I had two natures, my old nature always wants to please myself, and my new nature always wants to please the Lord.

Even though I was still a first grader, in many other ways, I was growing up. Our apartment had only one bedroom so mother got the bright idea to make the little dining room next to the kitchen, partitioned off by an archway, into a bedroom for me. It must have been a relief to my parents to get all my toys out of their bedroom. Daddy cut a heavy drapery rod to go across the top of the arch and mother made a heavy drape to go across it for privacy. Although I've had much nicer and even beautiful bedrooms in my lifetime, this bedroom was the most fun.

THE FAR EAST
BROADCASTING CO. (FEBC)

The Far East Broadcasting Co. (FEBC) was born in the same little church where the Lord had done a special work of His grace and salvation in my heart. John C. Broger, Robert H. Bowman and William J. Roberts were its founders. My parents were called to be their first missionaries. Rev. 3:8, "I know your deeds. Behold, I have put before you an open door which no one can shut because you have a little power and have kept my word and have not denied My name." (NASB) God was faithful to his promise.

For several years my dad's office was right in the church only a few miles from where we lived. Bill Roberts, one of F.E.B.C. founders, was also the pastor of our church. Pastor Roberts and his wife had a wonderful little daughter, Marilyn. Marilyn and I became best friends. Even to this day, it's hard for me to understand why Marilyn would have chosen to be with me when, in fact, she could have been very popular with all the other kids in church. The only reason I can figure out is she must have been a little angel from heaven sent to me. Of course, Marilyn and I had many things in common; first of all, our parents were in the ministry together. Marilyn was also the only child of her parents, just like me. We were the same age, my birthday in January, Marilyn's birthday in May. Marilyn was a "tomboy", only not as much as I. One Sunday, after church both our families went to a cafeteria for dinner. Somehow Marilyn and I got separated in line to get our food. By the time we got to our table, we discovered we both had ordered exactly the same kinds of food and our friendship was cemented even more than ever before. Although, Marilyn wasn't considered a handicapped at all, she wasn't really a strong little girl; she had to take naps just the same as me. She and I would sometimes take our naps together; we usually did more talking than sleeping. One Saturday afternoon, we were at a Sunday school picnic. Marilyn and I would just love to roll down the grassy slopes by the hour giggling all the time. We stopped for awhile to rest. A group of little boys about our age came over to where we were and began to make fun of my cerebral palsy, thinking they could influence Marilyn away from me. They received the shock of their lives when Marilyn reached down to the ground and pretended to pick up something to throw at them. "You get out of here." Marilyn shouted. Those little boys disappeared like a streak of lightening. I told Marilyn it was all right if she would like to go play with those other kids. My parents had always taught me to accept myself as a handicapped person, realizing that the other kids had every right to go and do what they were able to do. Marilyn, on the other hand, was a very unusual kid. She looked at me with real hurt in her eyes; it actually made me ashamed of myself that I had said a word. "Kay," Marilyn said, "I know perfectly well I could go play with those other kids, but I'd rather be with you." This experience with Marilyn I have reflected upon many times. To me it seems to be pictorial of a type of Christ. Our Lord Jesus says to those who are rejected or hurting, in paraphrase, though all others will turn away, "I will never leave you" "I love you just the way you are and I want to be with you." "I will never leave thee, nor forsake thee." Hebrews 13:5 (KJV) "Lo, I am with you, always, even to the end of the age." Matt. 28:20 (NASB)

(Bottom right, clockwise: Marilyn, Kay, cousins Donna and Margaret, and three friends. Birthday party for Kay).

Sometimes it was hard for us kids not to get the giggles in church, especially if the lady sitting across from us had a funny looking hat on. A few times while Marilyn's dad would be preaching it would be necessary for him to look down at us kids with eyes which told us we better be good. Marilyn and I would sometimes like to slide down the banisters outside in front of the church. Never once did I stop to think something which might be all right for her to do might not always be the wiser thing for me to do. It was easy, the way the banister was shaped, and it fit our little bottoms just perfectly. Sliding down the banister was easy even with my heavy leg braces on, it was jumping off down at the bottom which presented a problem but never once did I fall. All little children have guardian angels, my angel occasionally had to work overtime. Ps. 91.11, "He will give his angels charge concerning you, lest you strike your foot against a stone." Nothing, not even leg braces, kept me from doing what I was determined in my mind to do. Many times mother and I have discussed the fact that if I hadn't been handicapped she would have had a lot more to worry about. If my being cerebral palsy is the very reason for my soul's salvation, then certainly, it has been a plus in my life and not something to wish hadn't been. Matt. 18:9, "If your eye cause you to stumble pluck it out and throw it from you. It is better for you to enter life with one eye than having two eyes to be cast into the hell of fire." Most importantly, it must be a spiritual surgery of the heart. The apostle Paul wrote of himself: 2Cor. 12:7, 8, 9, "...there was given me a thorn in the flesh, a messenger of Satan to buffet me - to keep me from exalting myself. Concerning this I entreated the Lord three times that it might depart from me. And He has said to me, "My grace is sufficient for you, for power is perfected in weakness, most gladly, therefore, I will rather boast about my weaknesses, that the power of Christ may dwell in me." Ps. 119:71, "It is good for me that I was afflicted, that I may learn thy statutes." (NASB) CORRUPTIBLE EARTH? INCORRUPTIBLE CROWN.

MORE WITH GRANDPA WATKINS

Once in a while, mother and dad would be invited to functions where children weren't invited. Those were times grandpa would stay with me. I always enjoyed grandpa's fried potatoes. He would always burn just a few of them and would tell me it was just an accident that he burned 'em, but I still think he did it on purpose because they were oh, so good. By the time I got through eating all those friend potatoes, one fine spring evening, my front tooth was so loose it was just hanging by a thread. It had been getting more and more loose all day at school. Grandpa went searching all over the apartment trying to find my dad's pliers; when the instrument was finally found, the operation began. Grandpa put a dish towel in between the mouth of the pliers and proceeded to yank out my baby tooth. He called himself Dr. Burney just to make me laugh. He then gave me a half a lemon with sugar on it as cleansing. I have no idea how other kids experience this exciting time of getting rid of their first baby tooth, but I thought my grandpa to be a very clever man. I wish now I could have asked him if this was the same method he used with each one of his own twelve children. I'm sure the lemon was good for me, I'm not sure about the sugar. Much to my glee, I had been visited during the night by the good fairy that left me two dimes and one penny under my pillow. The next day grandpa took me across the boulevard to the corner drug store where I was able to buy an ice cream cone for only ten cents, those were the good ol' days. I still had eleven cents to put away in my piggy bank for a missionary project in Sunday school. It seems I could never eat an ice cream cone without making a mess. The more I worried about it, the worse mess it became. Grandpa was always so patient and long suffering with me. Grandpa decided the best thing to do was to just hurry home with the ice cream. Grandpa would then sit me down in a big over stuffed armchair, put a giant sized dishtowel around my neck and tell me to just enjoy myself; he would clean up the mess. Enjoying myself is something I always knew how to do. Grandpa told me to eat the cone half way down because the druggist puts his dirty hands on the lower part of the cone. This was humorous to me because in some ways grandpa wasn't always real clean in the way he kept his own person or rented room. He had no wife to encourage him to be any other way. In some ways, grandpa was a discouraged man because of the divorce.

However, there were some rules laid down by grandpa for cleanliness and safety, which had to be obeyed. For instance, never carry scissors with the point up. Always carry scissors with the point down. One day, grandpa caught me picking up something very dirty from off the ground. He scolded me, "You kids pick up the dirtiest things," grandpa said. I was very ashamed of myself;

whatever it was I held tight in my little fist, I dropped it like a hot potato. I always wanted grandpa to think I was a nice person even if I was handicapped. It softened the blow just a little bit that grandpa included me with the other kids.

Once my Aunt Katie told me she and grandpa were discussing me and grandpa said, "I don't understand what's wrong with that kid, but I'd sure like to help her." My Aunt Katie has a crippled leg. One shoe is built up about two or three inches. She and I always had a special understanding between each other. I thought it was just darling that she would tell me what grandpa had said. Now that I'm grown up, I have wished many times that I could have expressed to grandpa just how much he really did help me. For so many years I was very young and immature. I wish grandpa could be here now to read this tribute to him. Perhaps an angel up in heaven will whisper something in his ear. In grandpa's youth, there wasn't hardly anything known about cerebral palsy. If a CP person was seen going down the street, perhaps most people would think that person had polio. I remember when somebody asked me if I had polio. We were traveling across the United States on a deputation trip for the Far East Broadcasting Co. On the way home, we stopped in Chicago to visit friends. A very concerned lady asked me, "When did you get Polio?" I told her, "I don't have Polio, I'm Cerebral Palsy." She looked at me as if I were trying to evade the real truth. I tried to tell her that Cerebral Palsy is an injury to the motor part of the brain. I worried for days thinking I had done a stupid job of explaining myself. The following Christmas and for every Christmas thereafter, this dear lady sent me a Christmas card with a long friendly letter and five dollars. Mrs. Baumsgarden is gone now after suffering a long time with cancer. I really do miss her.

Although grandpa was a Catholic, he never went to church. Only once do I remember seeing grandpa all dressed up. Once, far in advance of this story, we received a surprise telephone call from my Aunt Julia. Her husband, Uncle Doc, was having some chest pains at work and left for his doctor's office a few blocks away. While he was there, he had a massive heart attack and died. It was a shock to the whole family. Of course everyone knew Uncle Doc was a workaholic, gone night and day away from his family.

One family joke is that it takes a wedding or a funeral to get us all together again. By the time all the aunts and uncles and cousins with their families have gathered together, we could almost form our own congregation, family friends just have to squeeze in where ever they can. At Uncle Doc's funeral, grandpa was there. He was all dressed up in a dark navy blue business suit, his hair was cut and his shoes were polished to a very high sheen. He looked like a Philadelphia lawyer. I was so proud of him I could have busted all my buttons. That's my grandpa I thought to myself.

One of my favorite bedtime stories was Heidi. I always had a special feeling for Heidi because I felt she loved her grandfather the way I loved mine. Of course, I had my very own precious parents, but in my childish imagination, I felt that if for some reason I were to loose mother and dad certainly grandpa and I would get along just fine.

29

Our moving into Los Angeles, in no way prevented grandpa from coming to see us, at least about once or twice a week. He would get on the bus in Inglewood, transfer to a street car in downtown Los Angeles, then take another bus to our apartment. Once in downtown, while waiting for the next bus, grandpa saw a homeless man in need of a coat. It was in the middle of winter, grandpa got right back on the streetcar again, went clear back home to Inglewood to get one of his own coats to bring back to the man on the street. Grandpa was always very tender hearted towards those in need of help. Perhaps this is why he was so loving and kind to me. When he came to see us, he always had his coat pockets filled with candy. He would give me permission to go into his pockets and select any candy I wanted, but to be sure to leave enough candy for the poor little kids down the street. I learned not only from my parents but also from grandpa, to think of someone else beside myself.

Grandpa would sometimes take me for a ride in my little red wagon. Once or twice I got him to take me clear down to Echo Park, several blocks away from where we lived. Grandpa was getting much older by then, I know he would much more have preferred to stay home in his favorite arm chair reading the newspaper, but he just wanted to make me happy. Our small apartment had only one bedroom which was given to me. Mother and Dad slept in the living room on a roll-a-way bed. Poor little grandpa had to go all the way home to Inglewood at night which wasn't always the safest thing in the world to do.

Grandpa showed me how he kept his little bundle of money in the sock of his shoe. He also carried a rock tied in a sock. He kept it in his pocket. He called it his "shalaylee." I think he just wanted to make me laugh. Grandpa never really ever though he would have to use it. However, one day he came home to us with a knife slit in his overcoat. We were thankful Grandpa wasn't hurt, but Grandpa seemed more worried about his expensive overcoat then the fact he could have lost his life.

I WAS A LUCKY KID

To neglect writing about the Orthopedic Hospital of Los Angeles and Dr. Kenneth Jacques would be failing in the acknowledgement of a very large portion of our Lord's providence and provision in my physical and spiritual life. The range of age for me during this time must have been between seven and ten. I can still remember our very first appointment with Dr. Jacques. I really didn't have any special feeling for him except I thought he was good looking, tall, dark, and handsome. He wanted me to walk for him. He ordered leg braces for me immediately. Three years was the regional stated order, which to me seemed like forever. With each additional six months, the time span of wearing my braces turned out to be five years. I was still quite a lucky kid.

Every day at school, I would see little children with full length leg braces, locked at the knees and with a pelvic belt, which was sometimes difficult to conceal under clothing, especially if a child was being lifted from a wheelchair onto the school bus. Usually the most severely handicapped kids were the smartest kids in school. It would always amaze me how these kids would always be at the top of the class when they didn't even have to do homework. Their high intelligence made up the difference for what their bodies would not do. These kids were always very good natured, always with a ready smile or even sometimes a giggle or two. Although Roy Rogers and Dale Evans were my favorite western stars, these kids at school were my real heroes.

The purpose of my wearing braces for a while was to plant my feet firmly on the ground, instead of striking out aimlessly and just hoping for the very best. Spiritually speaking I have always felt the need for our precious Lord to plant my feet on higher ground, "a higher place than I have known." Even better still, to be given "hinds feet" to climb mountains of adversity and survey this CORRUPTIBLE Earth with a spiritual perspective, looking beyond to an INCORRUPTIBLE CROWN by His mercy, grace and love. Ps18:33, "He makes my feet like Hinds' feet."

Before going to the brace shop, it was necessary for mom and I to go out to buy new high top shoes that would be able to accept a steel bar. Going to the brace shop was a new and exciting experience for me. I saw kids at school with braces but it never entered my head I would be wearing short braces myself. Swinging open the brace shop door for the very first time was an experience which would repeat itself many times as a growing child. I was glad the brace man had a smile on his face. He set me up on a very large table, put a giant size white paper under both my legs and with a utility pencil began to trace the shape of my legs onto the paper. It would be three weeks before my braces made especially for me would be finished. Before we could realize it, the weeks had gone by. Our old fashioned telephone rang, the receiver danced around on the hook, so it seemed, as if it could hardly wait to be answered. The pleasant and yet seemingly sinister voice on the other end of the line said, "Katherine's braces are ready." This meant another long trip for mother into Los Angeles. She would pick me up at school before going to the brace shop which was only about a block away from the Orthopedic Hospital. At the brace shop, the brace man brought in my new braces, the steal bars were so shiny they almost hurt my eyes. The man kindly put me down on the ground and asked me to walk. Right away, I felt I had lost my freedom to walk just anyway I wanted to, as the braces were restraining me and forcing me to walk correctly. In our Christian lives we need a restraint, the Bible, so we can learn to walk in His way. Ps 119:105 (NASB) "Thy word is a lamp to my feet and a light to my path." After all transactions were taken care of at the brace shop, it was too late to get back to school. I was already behind in my studies.

For the standard of living in those days, my leg braces were very expensive. The Far East Broadcasting Co was still in its infancy. Daddy was office manager, and most often he would pay office employees and field missionaries before he would take for himself. But the Lord was faithful to us through the difficult times. This was during the years right after Pearl Harbor when even the average family had difficult times knowing just what to do for the rest of the month at the end of their money. The kids at school would sometimes sing on the school bus, "I'll be down to get you in a wheelchair honey, braces and crutches cost too much money." Mother and I are so very grateful to our Lord for the faithful husband and father He has given us. Dad has always been willing to shoulder his responsibilities even under difficult circumstances. This is the way things are when the Lord Jesus Christ is given first place in the home.

MORE FAMILY AND FRIENDS

One day mother and I were taking a walk down Centinella Blvd. in front of our apartment, when we noticed a lady coming down the street with her CP daughter. We stopped to talk awhile, and come to find out they were neighbors, living just a few blocks away, in fact, on the same street as my Uncle Harry and Aunt Katie. Uncle Harry, you remember is the one who said I could punch him in the chin if I would take my first step. Aunt Katie is the one who told me what grandpa had said. Mrs. Blissard was a single parent with two other little girls besides Diana, who was the oldest with CP. Mother began giving Diana physical therapy along with me; mother also made arrangements right away at the Orthopedic Hospital for Diana to have surgery on her club feet. After Diana's recuperation from surgery, she began going with me to Washington Boulevard on the school bus. One day Diana's father decided it was just too much for him to remain faithful to his family so he took off with another woman. I was able to learn at a very early age to be thankful for my many blessings.

The first Sunday back at church I thought sure my faithful friend Marilynn would make some remark about my sparkling new leg braces but instead it seemed as if she didn't even notice them; our friendship continued just the same as before. It only took less than a week or ten days for the newness of having leg braces to wear off. The daily monotonous routine of putting them on in the morning, taking them off at night, besides repeating this procedure several times a week at school for PT, all began to settle in on me. The braces were very hot in the summer, something like wearing knee high winter boots in 95 degree weather which must have meant they kept me very warm on those cold winter mornings going to school. They say there's a good side to everything if we only look for it.

At the Orthopedic hospital clinic my physical condition was evaluated. They said, "By the time Kay has reached the age of twenty-one, people will hardly notice she's CP except for when she gets tired." This was good news for my parents, however, a tremendous challenge did still lie ahead for me. Some Christian people told me, "Kay, the Lord is going to completely heal you some day." One very well meaning saint of the Lord told my mother, "If I had a child like yours, I'd be on my knees day and night begging God to heal her." Although we appreciated the concern of the person, the Lord seemed to give mother the spiritual discernment to know there had to be a much better way. It seems from my own observation when people teach it's always the Lord's will to heal, they become very discouraged if He doesn't exactly do what they want Him to do thinking if they were just more spiritual or if they had more faith they would receive what they desire. When we truly believe Romans 8:28, "And we know that God causes all things to work together for good to those who love God, to those who are called according to His purpose," (NASB) this brings peace and reassurance that everything is in His control. When we truly believe all things work together for good to those who love our Lord, then even a miracle is not ruled out as a possibility.

MORE GROWING UP

Once in a while, mother would allow me to go a few hours or even a full day without wearing my braces. Every precious moment of that time as I recall I was in my cowboy boots. I loved those boots the way some children love their favorite blanket. I could hardly walk in 'em, the heels were too high for me, but I walked in 'em anyway. By the time I grew out of those boots they were so run over and twisted out of shape, even if I had brothers and sisters, those boots were certainly in no shape to give away as hand-me-downs. Even as an older child I was still a tomboy sometimes even to the discouragement of my mother. One day when mother had given up everything but hope of my ever transforming into a girl instead of a tomboy she said to me, "I almost bought you boys pajamas." That would have been perfectly all right with me. Looking back on it now, I marvel at the grace of our Lord to work even in the maturing of a person like me. It's my desire, now, to be the kind of woman God created me to be, not only in appearance, but most important of all, in the heart.

Being the only child as I am, mother asked my dad it he ever missed not having a son? Daddy answered, "To be honest about it, Kay is all the boy I would ever want; certainly she's all the boy I could ever handle."

Although I was much better off physically than most of the other children in school, I felt my PT therapist was trying to show some sort of understanding for me when she called my leg braces, CLOD HOPPERS. It seems as though I can still hear her say, as we would pass each other in the school hallway going in the opposite direction, "Go on into therapy, Kay, and get your clod hoppers off." It was always easier to take my braces off than to put them back on again. Sometimes my therapist would talk to me as if I were a much older person. She would tell me how by her professional skills she was able to know almost right away if a child should have been walking on their own without crutches or some other type of aid long ago. Because of fear or some other psychological problem, the progress wished for as yet had not been reached. If a child is suffering under stressful problems at home, such as the divorce of parents it can actually bring hindrance to a child having the courage to take the very important first step. My therapist would also be able to know if a child never really would be able to walk no matter how hard he or she would try. Many times I have seen a glistening tear or beads of perspiration on the brow of a youngster struggling to take just a few steps in the parallel bar. All these things have helped to instill in me a very thankful heart.

After therapy would be over, it was time to put braces back on again. My therapist would never offer to help me. I guess she was teaching me to be self reliant, not that I didn't realize I could put them back on myself, but to my own point of view, valuable time was being taken away from the classroom. First of all my high top shoes had to be laced up and a bow had to be tied. If I failed the first time to tie a bow, I had to try again. Meanwhile, the big ol' clock on the wall kept ticking away, then a strap had to be buckled across both ankles and the steel bars. "Why doesn't my therapist ever try to help me," I grumbled to myself. I tried to tell myself that most of the other kids in school had a lot more problems than I did but this didn't seem to help very much, I grumbled anyway. The actual brace part just below the knee-cap had to be laced up too. It seems the brace man never did give me enough shoelace to work with. I had to redo it several times before getting it just right. By the time I got back to class I would usually be exhausted and it was difficult to concentrate on my studies. My greatest hindrance in school was my inability to put my thoughts down on paper.

There was a certain girl in school who without any thought has made a lasting imprint upon my mind. To the outward appearance she seemed to be a very normal child. Her speech was perfect, the coordination of her hands was very good even her walking didn't really seem to be abnormal yet she had to have some physical disability or else she certainly wouldn't be coming to Washington Boulevard. Most of us kids in school wouldn't be able to hide our physical condition even if we tried. One day my curiosity just got the better of me concerning this person and I asked her what was her disability. I could hardly believe I would do such a thing. She told me, "I used to tell everybody, but now I don't tell anybody." As I laid my head on my pillow that night, it was hard to go right to sleep as my thoughts turned over the events of the day and the girl I had talked to. She had seemed so hidden and withdrawn even from the other children. Somebody must have hurt her very deeply, there was no other explanation. The thing that really bothered me the most is that she said, "I used to tell everybody." Several weeks later, one of the other children found out the mystery about this unusual girl. Both her legs were artificial. I stayed awake again another night. I tried to imagine what must have been going through this girl's mind when I asked her what her problem was. Perhaps she was thinking, "I wouldn't mind at all to wear leg braces like Kay if only I could have my very own legs. Some very wise person once said, I felt bad I had no shoes until I saw a person who had no feet. Truly this is a CORRUPTIBLE EARTH filled with sorrow, pain and disappointment. Phil. 3:10, "That I may know Him and the fellowship of His sufferings, being conformed to his death; an in order that I may attain to the resurrection from the dead." Through his sufferings we've been made partakers of eternal life where there will be no sorrow, pain or disappointment. CORRUPTIBLE EARTH, INCORRUPTIBLE CROWN

To the best of my recollection, by this time in my development I must have been in the third grade. Our teacher Miss Hall was a strong Christian believer. She enjoyed hearing Bob Bowman sing on the Haven of Rest radio program during those early days. Her own dad had been a hymn writer during his lifetime. She would also listen to Pastor Roberts in his daily radio program (Marilynn's dad). Although I was going through many personal struggles during this time, it was a comfort just to know Miss Hall was our teacher. If more Christian young people would consider handicapped children as a field of missionary service to go into, how wonderful it would be. As a special education teacher, it was Miss Hall's responsibility to understand each child's disability as well as to teach reading, writing and arithmetic. Miss Hall knew how to make learning very interesting. She set up a miniature grocery store in our classroom where we could learn to buy and sell. The cash register, the canned goods, even the paper bags were all mini-size. It was just darling. One day we made yeast biscuits. Mrs. Shaw (the head cook) let us bake our biscuits in the school kitchen oven. The school cafeteria was also our auditorium. It had a very large stage. I don't think I'll ever forget as long as I live the time when the eighth grade put on a play depicting the pioneer days of America. Act IV, final act, was a covered wagon going across the open prairie. The covered wagon was three wheelchairs tied together with rope, they were old fashioned wooden ones with very high backs, an old bed sheet was thrown over the top and tied at all four ends in knots to form a cover. The poor little covered wagon could hardly make it across the stage but somebody in eighth grade had a brilliant idea. As I sat close to the front with the rest of my class, the thought crossed my mind that perhaps the kids in regular school could never make a covered wagon because they don't have any wheelchairs.

By this time the words, Special School, began to take on a much broader meaning for me. Back in the second grade a dairy farmer came to school. He showed us how to make cottage cheese and buttermilk. This was one time when even a cow had to go to school. We were also taught how to milk the cow.

In every way Washington Blvd School was just like any other school except that it was for physically handicapped children. In fact, I personally felt Washington was letting down their standards when they opened up a classroom for the mentally retarded. It wasn't until my adult life when we were having a picnic in the park, I saw two retarded girls, ladies, actually, as they must have been a few years older than I. Smugly I thought to myself, "at least I don't have to be like them." I was having a difficult time walking over the rough ground at the park. Those two precious retarded girls came over to me and asked if they could help me. I wanted to laugh and cry all at the same time but managed to keep my composure. Here I was thinking I was so much superior to them but they were trying to think how they could help me. Now I see the mentally challenged in a completely different light. Now I certainly realize what Dale Evans Rogers meant when she wrote, *Angel Unaware*. They do have a lot to contribute to our world; most of all, their unconditional love.

Holidays were always a very special time at Washington Blvd. School. The Shriners and the Boosters came every year to give us parties, Halloween, Christmas and Easter. Although the Shriners have done much to help handicapped children with the Shriners Hospital, to my point of view, the Boosters always gave a much better party. The Shriners came on Thursday afternoon and the Boosters on Friday afternoon. Every Christmas the school bus drivers came into the auditorium to decorate the Christmas tree which reached clear to the ceiling.

Good ol' Santa always gave extra presents to the poorest child in school with a small Christmas tree to take home. One year the youngster with the Christmas tree just happened to be on our bus. With school books, crutches and Christmas presents, even the tree got home safely.

Easter was special because of our Easter bonnet parade. There was first, second and third prizes given out to the classroom with the most beautiful bonnets. The outdoor loud speakers would play, *In Her Easter Bonnet*. Surrounding neighbors would come out of their apartment houses to watch our Easter parade. If a child was in a wheelchair or on crutches, it just made him or her that much more in style. However, it's sometimes hard to keep one's Easter bonnet on straight when two hands are needed for crutches. Our third grade class won second prize, not that we kids were so smart, but Miss Hall was a gifted teacher and gave us lots of help. First prize went to the eighth grade. We were always proud of the eighth grade. They were the big kids.

In all my childhood remembrances, how could I ever forget Miss Carmire, our occupational therapist? Although Miss Carmire was a very nice person, we children never saw her smile. Once another girl and I got into an argument as children sometimes do. In the heat of the argument we decided to mimic each other's physical disability implying that neither one of us were doing as well as we should in our physical progress. When Miss Carmire saw what were doing, she began to laugh without restraint, her face began to flush from a pale pink to a deep red. We girls could hardly believe our eyes and ears. It was such a thrill to us children to see Miss Carmire laughing so

45

whole-heartedly that we forgot all about our little argument and continued our little show for the sole benefit of Miss Carmire. I realize now that I had a much better advantage than my friend because she was much more severely handicapped than I. Now I wish I could take her in my arms and hold her very close. My only consolation now is that we girls together were able to bring such delight to Miss Carmire.

Why do you talk so funny? Can't you walk straight? Those are words which if not accepted with the right attitude, not only can hurt but also damage a person's self image for life. Many times mother and I would take opportunity to explain what Cerebral Palsy was to children. Mother and I always believed children with inquisitive minds have every right to have their honest questions answered hoping that they would choose some humanitarian service as a career. Because of this more enlightened age in which we live, many with disabilities have been mainstreamed into society as productive citizens. With a healthy sense of humor, misunderstanding can be bridged. One little boy realizing my speech was different asked me if I were Swedish. Our neighbors next door were Swedish with a very heavy brogue. This little boy was staying with them for a while and somehow he made the connection between me and them. Even as a very small girl, I thought this to be funny; I never forgot it even until now. This is why I began this manuscript in the way I did on page one. Although I was much too young at the time to think up a wise crack, perhaps I should have said, "No, I'm not Swedish, I'm Cerebral Palsy."

Delores, a dear friend of mine, made a statement which to me seemed very profound and so true as she stood over me with her big beautiful brown eyes. Standing with her three footed canes, she said, "I'm not laughing at you, I'm laughing with you." There is a tremendous difference between laughing with someone and laughing at them. Perhaps there would be less chemical dependency in the world if we could learn the art of laughing at ourselves. Proverbs 17:22, "A joyful heart is good medicine." (NASB)

I could always count on Margaret and Harry, my two closer cousins, to laugh with me and to be my source of inspiration  during those long years of rehabilitation. Margaret and Harry were the delightful children of my Uncle Harry and Aunt Katie. When either of them would laugh at me, it was to encourage me to do better because they knew I could do better. In the very early days when I was just hardly able to walk, Margaret would get a hold of me under one arm and Harry would be on the other side of me, and they would then run with me. My own legs would be flying in every direction sometimes not even touching the ground. I would be laughing and giggling with delight but could feel my energy being drained. My head would be thrown backwards; it would then be quite difficult to get it back up again. I discovered I could roll my head round to either side then erect it. Margaret would always make sure to ask if I were getting too tired. I would always answer, "No". Concerned, Margaret would ask, "Shall we go again?"

My answer would always be in the affirmative.

To the outward appearance it would seem that I was just being a good sport. However, the complete exhaustion suffered later wouldn't only work a hardship on myself, but also on those around me. "A false balance is an abomination to the Lord but a just weight is His delight". Proverbs 11.1 (NASB). As I'm growing older, I've had to learn to accept my limitations; trusting Him for the needed strength to do whatever He calls me to do. 1 Pet. 5:7 "Casting all your anxiety upon Him because He cares for you." It has always been difficult for me to acknowledge when I'm getting tired, especially if I'm having a good time. We only know true happiness when our own self-will is completely surrendered to His perfect will for our lives.

Being the only child as I was, it was so wonderful that I had those two kids, Margaret Ann and Harry, to look up to and admire. I always wanted to be just like them. It seems we could always figure out some game to play. Sometimes we would play "church". Of course I was the preacher. I would tell them how Jesus came into my heart and took all my sins away. They told me I was much too young to be so serious. This didn't bother me at all because I knew Jesus did something wonderful inside my heart. Billy Graham said in his book, *Approaching Hoofbeats – The Four Horsemen of the Apocalypse*, "The Kingdom is already present in the lives of the believers who glorify Him by word and deed in the church and in society.

Just before television invaded our American homes and our whole way of living, radio was still the best way to spend an evening. Amos and Andy, Fibber Magee and Molly, were just a couple of my favorite programs. Radio was different than television in the way we could use and develop our own imaginations. Many times after school I would spend time in front of the radio listening to Stuart Hamlin's western show. Mother didn't always approve of my listening to his show because he would sometimes say things that weren't what we would consider "Christian". He would sing things like, "Lord, if you can't help me then please don't help that bear." Of course we know now that the Lord had His hand on Stuart Hamlin's life. Because of Hamlin's commitment to Jesus Christ, we now sing so many of his beautiful songs, such as, "It Is No Secret What God Can Do."

One day not stopping to realize the hundreds or even thousands of fan letters a celebrity might receive, I wrote a personal letter to Stuart Hamlin telling him how much his radio program meant to me, with all the sincerity that could ever be in my heart. This was soon after Hamlin's wonderful; conversion to Jesus Christ. A spiritual awakening was being mightily felt in those early days of the Billy Graham Los Angeles Crusades. It was a tremendous testimony that God could work his redemptive Grace in the heart and life of a person such as Stuart Hamlin or anyone on the Hollywood movie scene. My parents took me to one of the Billy Graham tent meetings when they were quite certain Stuart Hamlin would be there singing and giving his testimony. I had pictured in my mind Stuart Hamlin as being a very tall handsome cowboy with a ruddy complexion. Billy Graham preached a soul convicting message, just the same as always. After the meeting, dad carried me up to the platform to shake hands with Stuart Hamlin. When I saw him, he wasn't at all what I had pictured in my mind. Perhaps his wife thought he was a handsome man, I hope she did, but I had another opinion. To add more injury to my disappointment, he seemed to not even remember receiving my letter. My heart was crushed to be sure. Even my leg braces didn't seem to make an impression on him.

After our return from the Philippines, which I will talk about later, we spent one summer at Winona Lake Bible Conference grounds, Indiana. The highlight of the whole summer season was the Youth for Christ International Conference. I never saw so many Christian young people all together in one place. One of the featured speakers and singers was Stuart Hamlin. Although I was very thankful for his testimony for Christ, it was hard for me to muster up any special feeling for him because of my experience as a little girl. However, as I was nineteen myself, I really did enjoy the Youth for Christ Conference.

Moving day. I remember it well because it was Halloween. As usual, the Shriners and the Boosters had come to school to give us Halloween parties. As I said before, the Booster parties always seem to be the most interesting and exciting because they brought more entertainment, clowns, acrobatic stunts, magic makers and lots of music. Even our teachers had Halloween costumes. Right in keeping with my own personality, mother dressed me up as a little Indian girl. The costume she bought was in a kit and came complete with even the feathered headdress. By the time the school bus came barreling down the highway to stop in front of our place, things had already been set in motion for our move into the "City of Angels". At first, it would seem this would be a very exciting time for me, moving. The Far East Broadcasting Co. had expanded its ministry to where it was necessary to move their office to a larger facility, closer into the Los Angeles Civic Center. Of course it seemed only logical that it would also be much closer to Washington Blvd. School. However, there was a re-arrangement in the bus system, and some of my other friends had already been transferred to the new Loman School for handicapped children in North Hollywood. Mrs. Adams, the Principal of Washington, called my mother to inform her that because of our move into Los Angeles, I would be transferred to Children's Hospital School on Sunset Blvd. just down a few miles from our apartment on Mohawk. The logic of this was hard to understand, as we were now living closer to Washington than ever before going to Children's Hospital School. Because of the strange school bus route, I would still be two hours on the bus going each way to and from school every day. Washington Blvd. School had been like a childhood dream come true only to fade away never to return again. I felt perhaps I had not appreciated Washington the way I should have. They say we don't always appreciate what we have until we loose it. In the Philippines, we learned the preciousness of water when the well ran dry.

To make a quotation from a little booklet, "*Single but not Alone,*" by Sandra Aldrich, "Reality never fits our dreams." But what God plans for us very often is far better than even our dreams. "For I know the plans I have for you, declares our Lord, plans to prosper you and not to harm you, plans to give you hope and a future." Jeremiah 29:11

Looking back upon it now, in retrospect, I realize it was a wonderful experience for me to have lived for a while in the inner city. Now I understand other children who only have the city streets as their playground. Of course, the city street corner in those days was a much safer place for a little child on their tricycle than it would be today. My parents always made sure I had every kind of toy that a child wanted especially those that would help my coordination.

CHILDREN'S HOSPITAL

One day, while out for a Sunday afternoon drive, dad took us in through the back part of Children's Hospital to see the little three room bungalow school for the handicapped children. A school for the physically handicapped, I thought to myself, but certainly not special in the same way Washington Blvd. had been very special. At this age I was just beginning to have enough experience to make evaluations and comparisons, this I did without any reservation.

Washington had been the kind of school which would cause even a "normal" child to wish they were handicapped just to be able to go there. However, everything seems to have its good points and other things which are, perhaps, not so good. Children's Hospital seemed to have the finest physical therapy department anywhere. They were fully equipped very much like a real gymnasium. In order for me to continue receiving intensive therapy during school hours, it was necessary for us to change our registration from Orthopedic Hospital to Children's. This meant saying a temporary good bye to Dr. Jacques. Little did any of us know that in the providence of the Lord, our paths would cross again. Just as Dr. Jacques would say, "God works in mysterious ways His wonders to perform," by William Cowper, English hymn writer.

Dr. Jones and Children's Hospital became my little world for a time. At the very mention of Dr. Jones, my physical therapist, Miss Williams in Orange County, where we now have our home of thirty-seven years, got a broad smile with the comment, "quite a gal, quite a gal." There was never a doubt at all that Dr. Jones, being a woman, could hold her own right up there with the very top qualified doctors. I could tell right away that Dr. Jones didn't want me to have to wear those clodhoppers (leg braces) any longer than necessary. By this time, I had gained a certain amount of stability in my walking, although once in a while, I would still come home from school with a skinned knee or two. The left brace was taken off and the right one left on for another year. Even the Children's Hospital brace was different. My parents felt it was a more sensible one than the kind I had before. This brace had two steal bars instead of just one. It seems the orthopedic brace pulled me over too much to one side. My hip is a little out of line even today because of it. Soon after the right brace had also been taken off, we had a surprise visit in the gym by Dr. Jones. I remember her as a very quiet sort of person perhaps because there was so much on her mind. She turned my shoes upside down so she could see the places where my shoes had worn down or worn over. I heard her whisper as she shook her head, "That will never change." Our Lord doesn't always see fit to completely heal, but that doesn't mean He never does complete a miracle. Many times our afflictions have some eternal purpose. CORRUPTIBLE EARTH, INCORRUPTIBLE CROWN.

I could never quite understand why Children's Hospital had such a wonderful Physical Therapy Department when their Occupational Therapy room wasn't anything more than just a hole in the wall. Something like our school out in the back. My OT therapist was very young and very pretty. She tried to make a hand brace out of plaster of paris to help me hold my pencil better. It was a clever idea, cost my parents a little money but never really worked too well.

The very best OT department was at the Orthopedic. It was like a handicraft heaven with every kind of tool imaginable to work with. Once a week, the Red Cross picked up a few of us kids at Washington Blvd. and took us to the Orthopedic OT. The time always went by very fast at the Orthopedic OT because it was so much fun. Mother always had to come and pick me up there. This meant I was a whole afternoon away from classroom studies. The only thing I liked about the school at Children's Hospital was the hot lunches. We kids in school were given the same food as the patients inside the hospital. It was very good even better than Washington Blvd. It was brought out to us every day on a very long cart. As far as our academic studies were concerned, the attitude of the teacher seemed to be these kids won't get very far in life anyway so why go through all the effort to teach them. After having an arithmetic book placed in front of me, I was more or less left to myself.

They say children in smaller schools get more attention but it isn't always true. Most of my education has been from my own determination and the encouragement of my parents.

55

VISITS TO THE MOUNTAINS

The San Bernardino Mountains, Camp Pivika; "I want my mamma." Just about the time we moved closer into civic center of Los Angeles, my Uncle Harry and Aunt Katie with their two children, Margaret Ann and Harry, moved up to Crestline in the San Bernardino mountains. It was nice for us, occasionally, to get away from city life to go visit them. I loved to be able to go places as long as I could still be with my parents. I was very much bonded to my parents even at an age when most children would be venturing out a little more on their own. Even if Mom and Dad were to leave me with someone else for just one night, made me feel very strange and insecure. Being the only child, all the love and devotion of my parents had been centered on me. From the Crippled Children's Society of Los Angeles, we found out about Pivika, the Easter Seal camp for handicapped children. Even though at this point, I couldn't even handle one night away from my parents, for some strange reason, I thought perhaps two weeks up at Pivika might be fun. There was much preparation needed to get me ready for two weeks at camp. There were two long lists of things required to take up to camp, such as a lumber jacket, three or four pairs of Levi jeans, two pairs of shorts, lots of t-shirts, a flashlight. A hundred and one different things to make two weeks up at Pivika camp very enjoyable. Mother had to sew my name into each piece of clothing and paste my name on every other article. It has been said before that the mother of one handicapped child can be compared to the mother of twelve children. Us L.A. kids were to leave on greyhound buses from the Crippled Children's Society. This seemed like great fun. Most of the children were from under privileged families. Just the thought of being able to spend two weeks in the fresh mountain air was something very special. Saying good-bye at our departing station seemed to be all right with me. Pivika camp, just like Washington Blvd. School, was one of those special kind of places which would cause any normal child to wish they were handicapped just to get to go there. After the first or second day up at camp I began to get homesick. Our cabin counselors did everything possible to make me very happy but it was all in vain. The head counselor told me, "Kay, I don't understand how you are even able to go to school." This made me feel very ashamed but I was still very homesick and no amount of lecturing was about to change it. Uncle Harry and Aunt Katie came to see me as I called them on the phone and told them I was very homesick. They came to see me, thinking it might help as they were living close by. Uncle Harry and Aunt Katie thought Pivika camp was the most wonderful place on the face of this earth for handicapped children. I knew it, also, but nothing would change the fact that I was homesick and wanted my mamma. Seeing Uncle Harry and Aunt Katie made me temporarily very happy but after they left I was homesick again.

Uncle Harry and Margaret Ann finally had to come and get me and take me to their place as I was still homesick, not that I didn't love them, I just wanted my mamma. It was a real shame, too, because all the other kids up at camp were having such a great time. My parents had to come and get me. I was certainly the loser.

One day Grandma invited me to stay a few days with her. I wanted to go, but yet I knew I would get homesick and sure enough I did. The terrible part about it was by then I was becoming an older child perhaps ten or eleven years old. My dear sweet grandma is the one who snapped me out of that homesick syndrome I was in. It shocked me that Grandma would talk to me so sternly but I will always love her deeply because of it.  Grandma said, "Listen here to me, Kay, Grandma has every right to enjoy her granddaughter once in awhile, now just snap out of this homesickness right away." I was able to stay several days with her; we had a wonderful time together. My Aunt Agnes came one day and took me down to the beach, but most of all it was just nice being with Grandma. I felt so free. Best of all, as a teenager I was able to go back up to camp a few more times and have a wonderful time with all my friends from school. One year, the girl in the bed next to me was very homesick. I thought to myself she must be from a very loving family like myself. I felt the Lord had allowed her to be the one next to me because more than anyone else I would certainly be the one to understand. When I told the other campers how I got homesick, they could hardly believe I would ever be that way. Although I felt deep understanding for this girl who was homesick, I was so thankful in my heart for the complete freedom I had then to enjoy all the activities of the camp like the nature hikes and swimming. I tried archery but I was too weak to even pull back the string on the bow. Handicrafts are a favorite of everyone.

One year at camp I noticed so many campers were weaving belts, I asked one of the counselors if she would teach me to weave a belt. After showing me how it was done she then let me try. She said, "Kay, I know you can do it perfectly in your mind but your hands just will not do it." This was a disappointment for me. It looked so easy and seemed to be a good pastime in between camp activities; they were so very pretty when finished. It's my smaller muscles which are more Cerebral Palsy. As I started back to my cabin or up to the lodge, no one had to push me in a wheelchair, for this I have been very thankful. I was on my own two feet. Our God is so good. When there wasn't camp fire ring at night, there was dancing and singing in the lodge. My parents didn't approve of my dancing at all, but I tried it anyway a few times just to see what it was like. It really was lots of fun.

Each cabin took their turn camping out overnight under the stars. We rolled up our sleeping bags and we were transported in the back of a pick up truck to another location away from Pivika camp. We cooked hamburgers out in the open with the smell of pine trees and fresh mountain air. In the evening we roasted marshmallows with Hershey bar candy in between two graham crackers. It was soooo good. We spent all night in our sleeping bags with our day clothes. Our nature hikes were always great fun too. I usually needed a counselor to help me over the rough ground. One of the counselors said I did better than a tight rope walker. Whatever a tight rope walker does when he's high in the air, I can do almost that good down on the ground. One of the girls in our cabin called me hop-a-long Kay. She said I sometimes hop when I walk. One of my physical therapists told me I walk like a sailor on board ship out on the high rolling sea. Sometimes when I talk, people have a hard time understanding what I say. This has always seemed strange to me because I always understand every word.

The year that I got homesick I told my therapist at Children's Hospital that she reminded me of one of my counselors up at camp. She said that it must have been her sister. When she told her sister about me, her sister told her about my getting so homesick. My therapist thought it to be so funny that I wouldn't tell her myself.

SHOPPING, BIMINI BATHS
AND NEW HOME... AND
GRANDPA BRONSON

After summer camp, it was usually time to go shopping for school clothes. Mother always believed that if a person is willing to spend more money and buy quality clothing, they hold up better in washing and it's more economical in the end instead of having always to buy new clothes. We bought most of my things in places like Bullocks department stores or J.W. Robinsons. Because of this, I was usually the best dressed kid in school. Shopping was very often a whole day affair. In my younger years, mother would very often pick me up and carry me when I became exhausted. Even with heavy leg braces on, mother would carry me for several blocks back to where the car was parked. As a result, mother's legs broke down and it was necessary for her to have a vein ligation. This was made possible through a friend connected with the medical college of surgeons. Mother had fourteen incisions made on both legs.

Once while shopping, I was sitting down waiting for mother as I frequently do because I get tired so easily, a Shriner, with his tall red velvety hat with black tassels, seeing my leg brace on the right side, came over to where I was sitting and wanted to know what school I went to. I told him Children's Hospital. He then asked, "Are you going back tonight?" I said, "No, I'm going back tomorrow." He seemed to think I was an actual patient in the hospital, not realizing that there was a school in back of the hospital for handicapped children. Perhaps, at first, he was wondering if I was from Washington Blvd. School.

Bimini Baths. "Sorry, we don't carry liability insurance to cover handicapped people who might want to use our swimming pool facilities." For the very first time, I experienced the sting of discrimination as a handicapped person. Things are beginning to change now in our society today. People are beginning to realize that when we consider the needs of other people, we also help ourselves. We were able to enjoy the therapeutic value of Bimini Baths several times before being turned away. Perhaps the owners and operators of those swimming pools are by this time experiencing physical disabilities themselves which would be greatly helped by getting into a pool. Although, all three of us were very disappointed, knowing we would never again be able to darken the doors of Bimini Baths, it seemed as though dad could always figure out some other way of showing mother and I a good time. My dad always enjoyed reading maps and was continually coming up with some new idea, to take us on a ride around the city, or through the country side, out around the sea shore, or up into the mountains. Perla Labrador, a dear friend from the Philippines, who I shall talk about later, once said, "Mr. Bronson, you know my country better than I do."

By this time we were feeling that we had just about our fill of apartment living. Up until now my parents wanted to stay free, to stay ready in the event the Lord would call us again to some distant mission field. As yet, it seemed that dad would for quite some time be needed in the F.E.B.C. home office. We began to pray as a family that the Lord would provide us with a home of our very own. Because of the missionary testimony of my parents, the Lord was able to touch the heart of a real estate man, who, himself, wasn't really all that religious. He said, I think I have just the right place for you. Of course, we knew the Lord had just the right place for us. When it was quite certain we would be able to get this dream house, Grandpa Bronson wrote and sent an insurance policy which my dad had begun to pay on before going to Eastern Europe as a missionary. While in Danzig, Poland, dad wrote to ask his father to please cancel the policy, but instead, Grandpa continued the payments on the policy and sent it to us to use for the down payment on our first home.

"I'm goin' to settle down and never more roam and make the San Fernando Valley my home," so goes the Western song. At long last, we were owners of a piece of the western pie, "out where the west begins and the sunset ends", with the wonderful feeling that no one ever again could "fence us in." Even the grass felt so good in between my toes. Of course, I had felt green grass in between my toes many times before, but somehow this grass was different, this grass belonged to us.

TWELVE

I was now almost twelve years old. I didn't seem to have any problem at all saying good-bye to Children's Hospital. At Loman School for handicapped children out in North Hollywood, I was reunited with some of my friends from Washington Blvd. School. They were transferred out to Loman School at the same time I was sent to Children's Hospital School. Johnny said to me one day, "Kay, I thought I would never see you again." Johnny was a dwarf boy with no hands and two twisted feet, but Johnny's personality and high intelligence would be the envy of the tallest man with two good hands and feet.

Loman School was still a brand new school named in honor of the beloved orthopedic physician, Dr. Loman. Because of Loman being a new school, I had to be put on a waiting list to get into it. Meanwhile, I was given a home teacher. This was a new experience for me. I always thought that home teachers were given to sick children. I couldn't have felt healthier. I realized how wonderful it was to be able to go to school. There are so many wonderful things to be learned from being together with other children, things that can't be learned from a text book.

Another new experience for me was having neighborhood playmates. There seemed to be about five or six kids who, at first, seemed to want to play with me. In fact, it seemed as though we played together quite nicely for several days. I felt completely accepted by them and for a short time was even able to forget myself that I was handicapped. Once while playing a game on the front lawn of our house, something happened which I shall never be able to explain to myself, let alone try to explain to someone else. Those kids jumped up just as if they smelled poison; they ran away and I never saw them again. Climbing the front steps entering the house, I felt so rejected and all alone, continuing on into my bedroom it was hard to fight back the tears. At first I felt rejected as a person, but then I remembered how Marilynn Roberts had been my friend. Then just as if it were a miracle, I was able to see some humor in the whole situation. Those stupid kids had been playing with me for almost a whole week before they realized there was something different about me.

If I had been poison, it would have been just as bad for them. It seemed to me that if I had been in their place, I would have run away a lot sooner than they did. However, my being able to see the humorous side of it didn't seem to ease the loneliness

Now as I've grown older, I realize that loneliness is one way, like pain, and grief, in which we can learn to know our Savior better. "Our light affliction which is but for a moment works for us a far more exceeding and internal weight of glory." 2 Cor. 4:17. However, this is sometimes hard to comprehend when you are only twelve years old.

During my time spent with the home teacher, I was studying about the gold rush days of America. We as a family were sent to Portland, Oregon, on a deputation trip for the Far East Broadcasting Co. We stopped at the old Sutters Fort in Sacramento, where there is so much California history. When we returned home from the trip, I was completely exhausted although we had a wonderful time. These exhaustive times have always been difficult for my parents to watch me go through, not knowing just what to do. The quietness of the San Fernando Valley in those days was perhaps something I would appreciate now at this age but back then it was almost more than I could handle. The San Fernando Valley, including Van Nuys and North Hollywood, during those days was considered more or less out in the country. Nowadays, it has become so built up around there it's become just another suburb of the greater Los Angeles area with all the congestion of city life. I had been used to the sounds of the city when we moved out to North Hollywood. Perhaps this contributed to my extreme loneliness. We decided it would be nice for us to have a pet, someone for us to love and we would get love in return. Just like our dream house, the Lord gave us our dog, Spot. As it turned out to be, we received more love in return from Spot. Spot and I seemed to have a private understanding together. I think she even knew I was handicapped. One time I remember coming home about midnight after being away all day since early morning. As we drove into the driveway, Spot was waiting patiently out on the front porch. After thoroughly inspecting the neighborhood, she had found her way home. Many times when Spot would accidentally get out of the back yard gate, the neighborhood children would sometimes find her and bring her home. They would carry her from the leg pits letting the rest of her body swing. She loved it. Out in North Hollywood, Spot had her first litter of puppies. Although they were so very cute and sweet they couldn't be compared with Spot. Everyone loved her and Spot loved everybody.

At long last the school principal, Mr. Hersh, called to notify us of an opening for me to enter Loman. Just like Washington Blvd School, Loman was very special in many other ways than just the simple fact that it was for handicapped children. Of course, the Boosters and the Shriners never came out to Loman on special holidays like at Washington. Nevertheless, in no way was Loman School just about ready to be left behind eating the dust. At Loman school we had our own Wheelchair Basketball team with its very own private coach. Our school colors were blue and gold. Whoo-ray, whoo-rah for Loman school. Anything would have been better than having to have a home teacher. But Loman school was a real delight to me. Best of all, was the very short bus ride. I was the last kid to be picked up in the morning and the first to be let off in the afternoon. This was a real treat for me, but it wasn't going to last very long. At school, Johnny Denike and I shared the same study desk table. We had been long time friends from Washington, long before Loman School was even a dream. One afternoon I made the biggest mistake of my whole life. I yelled goodbye to Johnny just before he was to go to his separate bus. A girl asked me if Johnny was my boy friend. I acknowledged to her that I did consider Johnny my boy friend. She went immediately and told Johnny what I had said. Johnny told her, I consider Kay a very good friend but she certainly isn't my "girl friend."

I found out later that this other girl had been out many times to visit Johnny at his ranch in Van Nuys, but she had nothing over on me. We had been out there, too. If my loneliness was ever to be disrupted, Johnny was determined to make my life as miserable as possible. I still believe he really liked me as a friend because all of his free time was spent teasing me about the blunder I had made. Even while Johnny was teasing me, I thought he was just adorable.

Adolescence is a difficult time of life for many children and I was certainly no exception to the rule. One thing that contributed to my extreme loneliness was the fact that I was too normal to feel very much a part of the handicapped world. On the other hand, I was considered too handicapped to compete with the average normal child my own age. I felt trapped in between not knowing which way to turn. "God grant me the serenity to accept the things I cannot change, courage to change the things I can and the wisdom to know the difference." This choice proverb took on a special meaning for me as I began growing older. Much to my regret as I look back on it now, I wasn't trusting the Lord in the way I should have, trying to figure out my own life only brought more frustration and tears. Isaiah 55:8 "For my thoughts are not your thoughts. Neither are your ways my ways declares the Lord. For as the heavens are higher than the earth, so are my ways higher than your ways. And my thoughts than your thoughts." Nothing else has been able to help through the potholes of life as successfully as knowing the precious word of God, the Bible.

Face to Face

Face to face with Christ my Savior
Face to face what will it be?

By Carrie E. Breck

"For momentary, light affliction is producing for us an eternal weight of glory far beyond all comparison, while we look not at the things which are seen, but at the things which are not seen; for the things which are seen are temporal, but the things which are not seen are eternal." 2 Cor. 4.17, 18 9 (NASB)

CORRUPTIBLE	INCORRUPTIBLE
EARTH?	CROWN.

Many people my age, who were raised in Christian homes, will remember sneaking off to the neighbors house to watch television when it was still very questionable whether or not Christians should have a TV in their home. After much debate, we decided that because I was handicapped, without brothers, sisters or neighborhood children to play with, perhaps it would be all right for us to have a little television. Some Christian friends of ours who owned a furniture store gave us a special price. Some people from our church in Inglewood also paid some money down on our first television and asked for their name not to be given. The TV fit into a little cart on wheels, so if any of our Christian friends came over who might be offended, we could very quickly roll it into a nearby closet. We forgot all about the TV antenna sticking up very conspicuously on the roof. With the TV and our dog, Spot, keeping me busy, I almost forgot I was handicapped. Certainly my loneliness greatly diminished.

One day my Aunt Katie telephoned to tell us grandpa was in the hospital with a heart attack. Grandpa had never been sick before except for when he had diphtheria as a little boy. At the hospital, mother asked grandpa if he knew how to get right with Jesus, he said he did. Fortunately, the Lord spared grandpa's life for several more years.

Personally, I didn't feel quite ready to let grandpa go.

BACK AT FEBC

Meanwhile, the Far East Broadcasting Co. was seeing the miracle hand of the Lord at work as the radio ministry of reaching millions of unreached peoples with the message of Christ's love began to grow. John Broger, who at the time was President of the company, and his wife, Dorothy, with a group of other missionaries, were chosen to be sent to Manila to start an overseas radio station which became known as Christian Radio City. In the not too distant future Christian Radio City, Manila, was to play a very important part in changing my whole perspective on Christian ministry in such a way that my life would never be the same again. But first of all, there was much molding and reshaping of my spiritual life that only the power of the Holy Spirit Himself could do. The home office by this time had moved from a hotel suite in downtown Los Angeles to an empty store front on Glendale Boulevard in the city of

Glendale, another suburb of Los Angeles. I'll never forget the FEBC pick up truck in back of the store building. One night I had a very bad dream. In this dream I had gotten into the truck alone. As I was driving down Glendale Blvd., each time there was a stop sign I crashed into five or ten cars ahead of me. When I awoke from the dream, I was so thankful that it wasn't real. I promised myself I would never drive anything again. As a young adult, my dad has occasionally taken me out into the desert to test my skills at driving. Dad told me I did very well but never have my parents had any real trouble with me about wanting to drive because of my having had that terrible dream.

While we were still living in North Hollywood, the Brogers had already returned from the Orient. They happened to notice that I wasn't developing as normal as I should have been for a person my age. Even Marilynn Roberts was beginning to grow up and leave me behind, although we were still very good friends and it will always be that way. Aunt Dorothy has suffered much of her life with a severe back injury because of the experience they had on board ship of going through a nightmarish typhoon. Aunt Dorothy said she remembers seeing the ceiling of their cabin become like the side of a wall; she was bodily thrown across the room. Back home again in Los Angeles, Aunt Dorothy was able to receive a tremendous amount of relief from pain through the skillful hands of a wonderful chiropractor. I'll never forget that evening when Uncle John and Aunt Dorothy came to see us to tell us about their chiropractor wondering if possibly he would be able to help me. At least it wouldn't hurt to have x-rays taken of my spine. It was so very touching to me that people outside my parents would care that much for me. I'm so sorry not to be able to remember the name of the very special person who helped me so much; however, I do remember him as an elderly man with a deep sympathy for people who need special help. The x-rays of my spinal cord showed a double S curvature with the vertebras at the top of the spine very disoriented. Once again, it was very touching to me that Uncle Bob and Aunt Eleanor Bowman (Vice President of FEBC and now President) would want to help pay for my treatments when they already had two children of their own. At first it was everyday that mother drove me to LA for my treatments after school. Then it was three times a week, then once or twice a month for that whole year.

During this time we received another telephone. It seems that our lives would be much less eventful if the phone didn't ring. This time it was a lady calling from the Crippled Children's Society in Los Angeles. It seemed my name had been chosen from a long list of names. Who knows where they got my name, perhaps it was because of Camp Pievika. The lady on the other end of the line said my name had been chosen to have my picture taken with the very beautiful Jane Russell for the benefit of handicapped children. I knew we were being very worldly even to have a television in our home; now I was even on my way to Universal Studios in Hollywood. I had known other children in school who had been used for publicity, but they had always seemed much more severely handicapped than me. They were called poster children. Our quiet home turned into one of excitement. The lady who called didn't even tell us how I should dress but mother and I knew it had to be something special. In my imagination I could see Jane Russell in a very beautiful evening gown just like in the movies. Mother and I went to Bullocks department store in down town Los Angeles. We got a beautiful blouse with a light blue taffeta skirt.

UNIVERSAL STUDIOS

Finally, the great day came when we arrived at Universal Studios. Driving through those giant sized gates was quite an experience. The lady who called us on the phone about a week before was there to meet us. As she got into the front seat of our car and sat down beside me, mother and I both noticed right away her disappointment that I wasn't as severely handicapped as she was counting upon. I had already known the rejection of those who felt I was too handicapped to participate with them, now I was feeling the displeasure of those who felt I wasn't handicapped enough to satisfy their desire for which to use me. There was another mother with her little boy who had long heavy steel braces waiting at the studio for us. We as a family have always had the joke that if I hold very still and keep my mouth shut, no one will ever know I'm handicapped. As Jane Russell entered the studio, she had on light gray ski pants with a black sweater that shot holes in all my day dreams about her wearing a long, beautiful evening dress, but she was still very beautiful. Even so there was just no doubt about it. She had just finished making a snow picture. Just before the pictures were taken for the purpose of helping the Crippled Children

Society, there didn't seem to be too much concern given to how I or the little boy looked for the picture, but when it concerned Jane, every single hair had to be kept in just the right place. If Jane so much as moved her head there was a special person right there to re-comb her hair. During the picture taking, the lady from the Crippled Children Society noticed a slight tension in my right foot so she just seemingly by accident, but on purpose, twisted my foot to a more extreme angle to make me look much more handicapped than I would look otherwise. This made me feel terrible and was completely unnecessary. I thought about my therapist, doctors and especially my parents who had worked so much with me to get me to the place where I didn't even need my leg braces any more. I also thought of my parents who had worked and prayed for this day when perhaps I wouldn't even be considered handicapped. Last, but not least, I thought about the public who sacrifices their dimes and dollars in hopes that a person like me can live a more normal life. What about them, don't they have a right to know their sacrifice is not in vain? It was very sad driving home that evening. I looked at mother. Could she be feeling what I was feeling, I wondered to myself? Having a handicapped child is much harder on the parents themselves than the handicapped child. Kids for the most part only think about the present, parents consider the future. CORRUPTIBLE EARTH? INCORRUPTIBLE CROWN.

It wasn't until I was a little older that the full realization of what it meant to be handicapped fully settled in on me. Submitting to the sovereignty of the Lord's will in my life has been a lifetime struggle.

Several weeks later, we were sent four or five copies of the pictures taken with Jane and sure enough there was my foot all twisted. It didn't really make me look more crippled, it just made me look stupid. I showed one of the pictures to my physical therapist at school. When she saw my foot twisted, she was about to get upset with me. I told her my foot was twisted that way deliberately, by accident, on purpose. Fortunately, she was able to believe me although she could hardly believe her ears. I could hardly believe my self what I was saying was actually true. Sarcastically I told her, "Well, if they had called us a year or more before they did, I would have still had my braces on. Perhaps to their point of view that would have made a better picture." I was thankful my therapist was able to understand my kind of humor but I could see she was still a little upset, not at me, but at Hollywood.

About this time, Johnny was still teasing the life out of me. I often wondered if I could have handled it better if I had been in a wheelchair. As it was, I had to face it square shouldered, on my own two feet. One day I was called into the principal's office. The thought went through my mind, now what did I do wrong. After entering Mr. Hersh's office, he asked me kindly if it would be possible for him to have one of my pictures with Jane Russell. I reassured him I'd bring it to school the next morning. I might have been more proud of Mr. Hersh asking me for my picture if it hadn't been for that ugly, twisted foot but I was just thankful to know I wasn't in some other kind of trouble. The next day I tried to sneak into the principal's office without being seen or heard. My intent was to quickly leave the picture on Mr. Hersh's desk, then get myself out of there. Mr. Hersh stopped me, right in my tracks. "Wait, Kay," he said, "Wait a minute." The minute seemed like an eternity, as he very slowly and carefully took the picture out of the manila envelope. Mr. Hersh said, "Thank you, Kay." I thought to myself, what a long time to have to wait just to receive a thank you. If he had said anything about the twisted foot, I would have had to explain myself. Fortunately, he didn't; I was free to go.

During this time my chiropractic treatments continued, we said nothing about them at school. One day, my physical therapist happened to notice the small lift in my right shoe put there by the chiropractor. She said nothing but respectfully placed it back into my shoe all the while I didn't say a word, but I'm sure I was holding my breath. For the most part, the medical profession doesn't approve of chiropractors. Some chiropractors are better than others. There is a danger of over manipulation of the spine. The Lord gave mother wonderful discernment in regards to this even to where we quit the chiropractor long before he actually wanted us to. The Lord gave my parents the reassurance that he would take care of me and to this very day I have a very strong back. We will always appreciate what the chiropractor did accomplish in giving me a feeling of well being, starting me on the road to becoming a normal teenager. We were so grateful to the Bowman's and the Brogers for the part they played in this stage of my development.

NORTH HOLLYWOOD
AND SPOT

Having our first home in No. Hollywood brought many moments of delight to carry with us for a lifetime. Looking back on it now, it was during those special times that Spot had her first litter of puppies. They were so cute and sweet; there was about five of them but to our point of view none of them could compare with their mother. My Aunt Katie and Uncle Harry took one of the puppies. Later in the story when we set sail for the Philippines, Spot went to live with her own off spring. Because of Spot being a Rat Terrier, Uncle Harry told us later that she went after the rats in their garage with a vengeance. By this he was trying to tell us Spot paid for her keep.

One of the advantages of a family having their own home, which is most important, seems to be, not having to pay rent. It seems I can still hear my dad say renting is like putting your money in someone else's pocket. It wasn't too long before the Far East Broadcasting Company realized the truth of this statement. They soon bought a large piece of property in Whittier, a town just the opposite end from where we lived in North Hollywood, which meant that we, too, would have to make another move. I remember those rides in the car that was necessary for dad to make every day to and from work. I wondered if dad ever remembered those two hour rides I had twice a day on the school bus. I knew from personal experience what dad was going through. It was difficult, at first, to leave North Hollywood. In many ways we felt as though we had already found our little pot of gold at the end of the rainbow. Also, it was hard for me to leave Loman School. Although Johnny Denike was teasing the life out of me, it was one of those situations where it was still hard to say good-bye. I often wondered what happened to Johnny. Did he ever go to college? Did he get married? Was he ever able to drive a car? If he ever did, was it a special one made just for him? These are questions I will carry with me to this life's end.

Just before I left Lomen School, Johnny was scheduled to have corrective surgery on both his twisted feet and also on his arm, which only had two fingers, so he could hold a pencil in between them. I always remember Johnny as having to use both his short arms to hold a pencil. Perhaps I wouldn't even care about those things if I wasn't handicapped myself. Sometimes our Lord allows us to go through sufferings, not only so we will learn to know Him better, Psalm 119.71, "It is good for me that I was afflicted, that I may learn Thy statutes," but also so we can comfort others better in their afflictions. Otherwise, our lives would be very self-centered. One of those statutes, which we learn about in Psalm 119.71, is that we learn to understand others because our Lord Jesus came to understand others and to heal.

Just the very thought of having to leave our home in North Hollywood, was very upsetting to me for a time. Being moved around a lot is just part of missionary life, however, it seems our Lord never asks us to give up anything that He doesn't replace with something as good, if not better. Neither did I realize that our experience in the Philippines was just around the corner, which would reshape my whole out look on life and bring a new dimension to my Christian experience. Jeremiah 29.11, "For I know the plans I have for you, declares the Lord, plans to prosper you and not harm you, to give you hope and a future." At this time, we didn't really even know if I would ever learn to read, as it was quite hard for me, or be able to express myself on paper. Now I realize that we can trust in the arms of our sovereign God. For His ways are perfect.

2 Peter 3.8, "...that with the Lord one day is as a thousand years, and a thousand years as one day."

AT HOME IN FULLERTON
CALIFORNIA

As I sit here at my electronic typewriter in our Fullerton home, it's hard to believe that we have lived here for almost forty years. Yet, in my memories, I'm able to take a nostalgic trip back to those early days when the house we now live in was nothing more than just a foundation with so much building yet to be done. Our hearts rejoice just to think of our heavenly Father as being the Master Builder of our lives. Ephesians 3.16-19, "…that He would grant you, according to the riches of His glory, to be strengthened with power through His Spirit in the inner man; so that Christ may dwell in your hearts through faith; and that you, being rooted and grounded in love, may be able to comprehend with all the saints what is the breadth and length and height and depth, and to know the love of Christ which surpasses knowledge, that you may be filled up to all the fullness of God." (NASB)

It seems life was much simpler in the years gone by, when folks took the time to appreciate the fragrance of orange blossoms, which filled the early evening air. As it is today, newcomers to this county ask the question, "Why was this area named Orange County?" As I recall growing up, it was so sad to see the orange trees allowed to die in order for housing developers and shopping malls to make a mint.

One advantage of seeing your own house being built from its foundation is having your own desires built into it. When our lives are in the hands of our heavenly Father, the Master Builder, He is able to work His plans out for us. CORRUPTIBLE EARTH, INCORRUPTIBLE CROWN. The Lord Jesus said, "I will build my church; and the gates of hell shall not prevail against it." Matt. 16.18

Even Spot seemed to like her new home.

Shortly after our move to Fullerton, we became charter members of Temple Baptist Church. This is where I received my foundational growth in the Word of God, which sustained me through the difficult teenage years. Mother remembers the time when I cried for three days, in the realization that I would always have my limitations as a handicapped person. Now I realize that I had to be broken both in heart and mind before the Lord would be able to produce His resurrected life in me.

The youth group at Temple Baptist accepted me in such a beautiful way, at times it seemed as if I was just as "normal" as they were. Sometimes I was even cornered into participating in the youth choir which made me nervous. One time our pastor's wife, Mrs. Hudson, asked if I was ready to commit my life and future into the Lord's Hands. I told her I didn't think I was ready yet. Now I realize the preciousness of our Lord, Who will not let us go.

CORRUPTIBLE EARTH, INCORRUPTIBLE CROWN.

Grandmother Bronson knew I was going through a spiritual battle and wrote a beautiful letter concerning the commitment of my life to the Lord. She told of a cerebral palsy girl who was completing her education in their Bible college and of her desire to be of service to the Lord. Grandma told me the Lord could work in my life the same way. This letter was saved and we still have it; I can see now the fulfillment of the faithful prayers of my grandparents.

Carl Harvey School for handicapped children was in Santa Ana, not really a long way from our home in Fullerton, yet, I had to leave home on the school bus at 7:30 in the morning and didn't get home 'til 4:30 in the late afternoon, a long hard day for a little cerebral palsy girl, to be sure. But somehow the Lord helped me through those difficult years. Although there were times of discouragement, I can look back on everything now and see the purpose of the Lord in all of it.

My first day at Carl Harvey School brought back a few unpleasant memories. I thought to myself, "Oh, no, another school like Children's Hospital." My heart sank deep into my shoes. This little two-room school house was hidden away in the back of Santa Ana's Elementary School. To be honest about it, I was beginning to feel just a little homesick for Lomen School. Thoughts of Johnny began to fill my mind. I remembered how, with only two fingers on one arm and a protruding bone out of his elbow on the other arm, Johnny had been able to play a few short tunes on the piano. With what we would call no hands at all, Johnny would take old, worn-out clocks apart and put them back together again. In spite of my already deciding that I was not going to like Carl Harvey School, the teacher gave lots of encouragement. When I told her just where I was in my schoolwork, she said, "Kay, you are so fortunate, because you will always be able to learn." "Some of these children will never be able to go any farther in school than the first grade. This teacher, I thought, was so very precious to open up to me this way, although I was still far behind in school for my age. There was even discussion about getting me into the regular public elementary school up in front of Carl Harvey. But back in those days handicapped children weren't as readily mainstreamed into the public schools as they are today. It was very difficult to find a teacher who would accept the responsibility of having a handicapped child in their classroom. A Methodist minister started Carl Harvey School. This was my first experience of having prayer in school. This little prayer was said at lunch time: "Father, we thank you for the world so sweet, we thank you for the food we eat, we thank you for the birds that sing, we thank you, God, for everything." Not much of a prayer in my way of thinking but it was better than nothing at all.

Because of my being a teenager, they sent me to a special class for handicapped children at Lathrop Jr. High School in Santa Ana. It certainly didn't reduce the long bus rides every day but as I look back on it now the Lord was so good to allow me the privilege to be in Mrs. Brown's class. She was able to give me lots of personal help with my studies and she did so much to help straighten out my thinking about myself and about life. Mrs. Brown always let me talk freely to her and she would always talk straight on to me. Mrs. Brown gave personal attention to each one of her fifteen students. Mrs. Brown, I do believe, was called by God to work with handicapped students the way some people are called into the ministry. She continued teaching the physically handicapped long after her husband had retired. Mrs. Brown didn't live very long after she finally retired. Physically handicapped children had been her whole purpose for living. Mrs. Brown started out as a home teacher. One day she got a bright idea. Wouldn't it be wonderful if all my students could have the wonderful experience of going to school? Lathrop Jr. High opened their hearts up to Mrs. Brown and gave her a room.

One day Mrs. Brown was taken to visit in a home where she found a little girl who had been in bed for eighteen years. Mrs. Brown fell head over heels in love with Beverly. "This girl needs to be tied securely in a wheelchair and brought to school," Mrs. Brown said. Often I have tried to imagine what it must have been like for Bev to be brought out into the fresh morning air for the very first time. At school, Bev began to talk to us. Being very severely handicapped with CP, she had never talked before in her entire life. With every effort to speak, Bev became a very important part of every conversation. Sometimes we knew Bev's point of view just by her giggle. The last time I heard of how Beverly was doing someone in our church who knew her, told us that Beverly had accepted the Lord as her own personal Savior and Lord. It just seems inconceivable to me that a bright person like Bev could have been neglected for so many years, perhaps by many who stopped long enough to say, "Oh what a pity", then turned and walked away. CORRUPTIBLE EARTH, INCORRUPTIBLE CROWN.

On another day, Mrs. Brown was invited to a Hollywood dinner where she had the privilege of sitting next to the very famous comedian, Bob Hope. In the course of conversation, Mrs. Brown asked, "Bob, after this dinner, would you be willing to go with me?" Strangely enough, Mr. Hope did follow Mrs. Brown all the way out to Carl Harvey School in Santa Ana. By this time Carl Harvey had its new building. For the very first time Bob Hope was seeing with his own eyes what it really is to be a child with CP. He was seeing frail little children with heavy steel back and leg braces. Being the very tender hearted person he was, he turned to Mrs. Brown and said, "Something must be done about this." Bob Hope went back to Hollywood a changed man. This was the beginning of the Bob Hope, "Thanks for the Memories," telethon specials for United Cerebral Palsy. It was a real blessing to each of us children when we were told it was originally our own beloved Mrs. Brown who made it all possible. There is a possibility that science will develop a cure which eliminates the RH negative factor in the mother's womb which most always results in a child being born with CP, however, there will always be accidents such as mine. We will forever be grateful that my injury at birth wasn't as severe as it could have been.

Another darling girl in Mrs. Brown's classroom, very similar to Beverly, was Helen. Helen said to Mrs. Brown one day, "I'm going to grow up to be a 'nobody'." Mrs. Brown very wisely answered, "If you're going to be a 'nobody' when you grow up, then be sure that you're the very best 'nobody' that you can be. Then she added, "You have to be a 'somebody' or else you can't be a 'nobody.' Mrs. Brown taught us this little poem:

I AM ONLY ONE

But what I can do, I should do,
And by the Grace of God, I will do it.

By Edward Hail

This is what Mrs. Brown called Cerebral Palsy perseverance.

If it hadn't been for Mrs. Brown, perhaps I wouldn't even be writing this testimony, but most of all, Mrs. Brown imparted to us her values for living. She wanted us to be the very best person we could be no matter the outcome of the future. When our departure date for the Orient was made known, Mrs. Brown told me she always wanted to be a missionary but for health reasons she wasn't able to go. The Lord gave her an open door of ministry that no man could shut. Rev. 3.8

Kids will be kids, so goes the old cliché. Being a handicapped child in no way hindered me from making this truth a reality, especially if I had my good friend, Marilyn Roberts by my side. By this time Marilyn and I were slowly developing into our teenage years. Tomboy tendencies gradually gave way to pin curls, nail polish and our favorite songs on the Hit Parade. Yet kids will be kids no matter what the age. Because of going to separate churches now, it would be even a year or more before we would see each other again. When we did get together, it seems we could always make up for lost time. Just like the time Marilynn came to spend a weekend with us. It seemed so good to have Marilyn with us, just like old times. On Sunday morning, Marilyn and I were let off at church on our own for whatever reason I don't recall, perhaps my parents had a deputation service for FEBC in some other local church. Getting through Sunday school seemed to be easy enough for us, however, the morning worship service seemed to be quite a different story. I looked at Marilyn; Marilyn looked at me with certain eyes, which most always meant something mischievous, was about to happen. Temple Baptist was a newly formed body of believers meeting in the Masonic Temple in the heart of downtown Fullerton. Just before service, Marilyn and I were able to casually sneak out a side door. Down the center of town we went looking in all the shop windows. We thought we were on easy street. I felt something in my pocket. It was the church-offering envelope. " Look, Marilyn, how are we going to explain this." In my thoughts, I was wondering what I would say if mother asked me if we had gotten a blessing from Pastor Hudson's sermon. I could say, "yes," but it wouldn't be the exact same truth she would want to hear. The only solution to the problem would be to hurry back to church. After many years of knowing me, Marilyn had learned that if she would take my hand, we could run together. By the time we got back to the church, they were already singing the Doxology. I just happened to know where the deaconess ladies were counting out the money upstairs. Marilyn waited for me at the top of the stairs as I sneaked around a side curtain, which opened into another room. I quickly handed the offering envelope to one of the ladies as her saucer like eyes penetrated deep into mine, questioning, "Kay, are you being a good girl"? I so wanted to be able to say, "Yes," but I knew in my heart the answer was, "No." Marilyn and I felt our little plotted scheme had worked all right once we were back outside. Marilyn said, "It's all right if you tell your mother what we did, but please don't tell mine". Over the many years, Marilyn had grown to love and have confidence in my mother. After being raised in a large family of twelve children mother had long since known that kids have to be kids or bust. Back at school on Monday morning I told Mrs. Brown what we kids had done. I thought sure she would be very ashamed of me but instead she just called me a very normal kid. When Marilyn and her husband graduated from Bible College, they went to Columbia as missionaries.

Summer vacation rolled around quickly and soon it was time to go back up to camp Pivika. My parents were always enthusiastic that I should go, making all the necessary preparations. Only one thing they asked of me as Christian parents, that I wouldn't participate in the dancing. Mother recalls the time before she came to Christ that her life was completely controlled by a spirit of dancing. Mother expressed it this way; "There was a time in her life when she would rather dance than eat." My parents' desire for me was always that my life would be separated unto the Lord.

I always wanted to be obedient to my parents however, when Raymond asked me to dance, I melted. It was just too much for me to say, 'no thank you.' Ray and I had been friends a long time in Mrs. Brown's class. Ray and I were just about the same type of CP. We were both so shaky we could hardly dance together. During the dancing, Ray said that mother told him he should take care of me. This was humorous to me. I thought to myself, "Ray, if you just take care of yourself, you'll be doing an excellent job".

As Ray relayed to me one day on the school bus at the age of twelve years old, he was a very normal, happy-go-lucky kid. He was getting top grades in school, his parents were very proud of him; he was the apple of their eye. Certainly Ray had a promising future. One day as he was turning the final corner on his bicycle before arriving home, suddenly, Ray was hit by a truck. The next thing Ray knew, he was in the Los Angeles Orthopedic Hospital. After many months of operations, physical therapy and full length leg braces, Ray would be categorically CP for the rest of his life.

I have often times wondered about the extreme adjustment it would have been for me or anyone to be struck down in mid-life, as so many are, to have all your hopes and dreams just crumble at your feet like shattered mosaic glass which once displayed its true colors. My CP has been so much a part of me since birth, it almost seems as if it were my nationality, being willing to surrender my own self will to the control of the Sovereignty of the One whose ways are much higher than mine.

TO YOU

Father it hurts to let go of my plans,
But fulfillment and joy come
in obedience to You.

By Betty Stam

My physical therapy by this time wasn't as vitally necessary as it had been in the earlier years. My parents always made it a point to give testimony to the healing touch of our Lord. Of course our parents, doctors and therapists deserve much more credit than they will ever receive on this earth, however, to overlook the intervention of a power much higher than human abilities is failure to acknowledge the very one who created us in the first place. There seemed to be only one problem left to give my therapist. Miss Williams' nervous frustration was the persistent twisting of my right foot when I walked. Miss Williams observed right away that my right hip was out of line. "You twist your hip before you twist your foot", Miss Williams said. "To my point of view the doctor should have ordered full length braces for you with a pelvic band. These doctors, Miss Williams said, never do know what to do unless we therapists tell them. Miss Williams was thinking out loud. She always knew she could trust me to see things objectively which seemed to be innate with most all handicapped children. It's only as we grow into adulthood and begin to be concerned about the future that depression sometimes overwhelms us. I know from personal experience this can only be overcome in the power of the Holy Spirit. We had opinions from two different doctors that if I didn't have an operation on my right foot, wearing a leg brace would be necessary for the rest of my life. After five years already of being in braces, it was much easier to consider an operation as the way to go. Mrs. Brown thought I was just too proud to wear a leg brace to school. She had never been told of my past history. Over the long years of my growing up, our confidence still remained in Dr. Kenneth Jacques more than any other doctor.

The possibility of having an operation may seem to have painted a cloudy picture, but the real truth of the matter was that our Lord, in His sovereign plan, was to perform something marvelous in our eyes. At long last we were beginning to see the light at the end of a very dark tunnel as far as my academic studies were concerned. I began to read with much enjoyment. Mrs. Brown called being able to read "arm chair traveling." My reading opened up new worlds for me. The Lord also provided for me in a miraculous way, an electric typewriter. It would delight me to see Mrs. Brown's eyes light up when I would bring to school on Monday morning two or three type written pages I had done at home on the weekend. Mrs. Brown immediately negotiated to get an electric typewriter for the classroom. This meant I was able to do all my studies at home and school, typewritten. When it was time for me to enter the Orthopedic Hospital for the surgery, it was with a happy heart knowing the past year at school had been a very successful one.

Previous to entering the Orthopedic, we made an appointment with Dr. Kenneth Jacques at his Wilshire Blvd. Office. Just to sit in his waiting room is such an inspiration. We saw on Dr. Jacques table a Bible, Gospels of John and Gospel tracts of all sorts. Our hearts leaped for joy within us. Something very wonderful must have happened to Dr. Jacques since the last time we had been in touch with him. Dr. Jacques' open and strong testimony was to be the turning point in my own commitment to the Lord Jesus. As is customary in a doctor's office, we were asked to fill out a questionnaire. When asked for occupation of father, my dad wrote down "missionary". When it was our turn to see the doctor, we could see the love of Christ shining through his eyes. Immediately he proceeded to tell the wonderful story of how he came to know Christ in a very personal way.

As the story goes, it seems Dr. Jacques always considered himself to be a Christian. He did all the right things, went to church every Sunday and was a very good American involved in every sort of humanitarian activity. Dr. Jacques donated his time once a month to helping handicapped children, especially CP children. Still there was deep down in his heart an emptiness and desire for lasting peace. One of Dr. Jacques' patients who happened to be an Evangelist missionary said, "Dr. Jacques, you doctors are rich, why don't you take a vacation and come with me on one of my trips into the high mountains of Mexico." Without any hesitation, Dr. Jacques said he would. Very high up into the primitive inaccessible mountains, after many hours of traveling by foot, they arrived at a little village church. Dr. Jacques was unable to understand a word of the language spoken in the little church with a thatched roof and mud floor, but somehow the power of the Holy Spirit touched the heart of Dr. Jacques one night and he knelt down in the mud to give his heart and life to Jesus Christ right along side those precious Indian people. For the first time, Dr. Jacques found the peace and joy he had been searching for all his life. As Dr. Jacques expressed it, "God works in wondrous ways, His miracles to perform." Dr. Jacques' life was completely changed. He still did all the right things but now with an eternal purpose.

In the hospital I observed how the faithful testimony of Dr. Jacques captured the attention of other doctors, nurses and interns. I remembered as a little girl, I had been very tender towards the things of the Lord. But I had somehow turned away from that simple child-like faith and began to try to figure life out for myself which only brought dissatisfaction and unrest. Deep down in my heart I wanted that joy and peace I had known even as a small child. I also admired the courage of Dr. Jacques, to take a stand for Christ when perhaps compromise would be the order of the day in a doctor's world. One night after surgery when the pain in my foot was too much for sleeping, I spent time with the Lord. I asked the Lord to take my life and make of it something that would honor Him.

I asked the Lord to make my life a witness for Him, to make my life Christ centered instead of self centered, to make my life count for eternity the way Dr. Jacques was allowing the Lord Jesus to use him. The peace and joy of the Lord flooded my whole being for the first time in many years. I thanked the Lord for the pain in my foot that kept me awake. I promised I would trust him completely for my life and future for only He is worthy of our full surrender. The word "Missionary" formed almost an indelible impression upon my thoughts. How stupid to even consider that a person like me could ever be a missionary. At this point in time, we had no idea that just one year into the future we would be setting up housekeeping in Manila, Philippines. Yet the word 'missionary' refused to leave my mind. I thought for sure after getting home from the hospital, the word 'missionary' or any silly thought of ever wanting to be one, would certainly vanish from me but instead the missionary call of the Lord became even stronger within me.

During the summer months of convalescence, I read the National Geographic magazine about many different countries and began praying for those people that somehow they would be reached with the gospel. Best of all, I began reading the Bible with understanding and committing scripture verses to memory. Mrs. Brown loaned me study books for the summer. When I did finally realize how far behind in school I was, I almost had an exhaustive collapse trying to make up for lost time. Back at school in September, I was far advanced of Mrs. Brown's little classroom for the handicapped. I asked her if she thought it would be possible for me to get into one of the mainstream classrooms of Lathrop Jr. High School. She seemed to think it was worth a try.

By then I had graduated from one full length and one short plaster cast to a brace on my right leg to be worn both day and night for one year. Getting used to the brace was no effort all. In fact, in many ways it just seemed like old times. The next day after my discussion with Mrs. Brown, upon entering her classroom, I saw written upon the drawing board, "Kay Bronson – first period social studies, second period – English."

The Lord had performed another miracle for me. My teacher, Mrs. Peterson, was a compassionate and understanding person. The other students accepted me the same as the teacher. This was another time when I completely forgot that I was handicapped. Mrs. Peterson's room was called a core class, social studies and English together, a new experiment in the Santa Ana school system. It was decided that I would only be graded on the work I was able to produce by the end of the school year. My study production had tripled and I was making A's and B's. I felt the Lord was showing me, it's no secret what He can do for us when our lives are committed to Him. One day at lunchtime, I told Mrs. Brown my experience with the Lord in the hospital. I also told her of my desire to be a missionary although I didn't fully understand the reason why.

THE MISSION

One evening my dad entered my bedroom while I was busy doing my homework. I noticed right away a very concerned look on his face that made me know there was something very serious on his mind. He had no way of knowing for sure how I would respond to what he was about to say but it's always better to come right out and say what's on your mind. My dad said, "Kay, I need to tell you that your mother and I have been asked by the FEBC to go to the Philippines as directors of the Christian Radio City, Manila. Are you willing to go with us?" The word missionary once again flashed into my mind. It was then my privilege to tell my precious parents something for some reason I hadn't gotten around to telling them before, how the Lord had dealt with me in the hospital about allowing Him to take complete control of my life. The Lord was beginning to weave a tapestry of our lives in such a way that only He could receive the glory. I told dad that He had made me ready and I was willing to go.

While I was still in the hospital, I happened to notice the girl in the bed across from me had very beautiful skin of a rich golden brown, though I knew she wasn't Hispanic. I also noticed Perla was receiving special privileges which weren't given to other patients. Perla's mother was able to visit her every day; the other patients were only able to see their parents on Thursday and Sunday out of the week. Perla also had a private night nurse for a few nights after her major surgery. One morning I heard Perla tell the night nurse to please not come back again, it was costing too much money. I thought to myself what could be so special about Perla Labrador.

The day after my surgery happened to be a Thursday. Mother and dad were able to visit me again. It was on this day we learned that Perla wasn't just any other person. Perla's father was the Chief Justice of the Supreme Court in the Philippines and Mrs. Labrador was the sister of President Magsaysay. Perla was at that time eighteen years old. As a small child she had been the victim of Polio. There in the Orthopedic ward Perla and I had many long conversations together. She told me of the day she was brought to the States on a stretcher only able to move her head. After eighteen operations, five of which were major, as Perla relayed it to me, she was then going in for her final surgery which would make it possible for her to walk a few steps on crutches. Dr. Loman was Perla 's doctor which was interesting to me because of my attending the Loman School in North Hollywood. Even though Perla had gotten quite used to our American way of life, to Perla's point of view, there was still no place like the Philippines and Perla would soon be going home.

Now, knowing for certain that we would be making Manila our home for a couple of years, was also the possibility of seeing Perla again.

Perla had a very brilliant mind. She was already a graduate of the University of the Philippines. To Perla, figuring out mathematical problems in her head was as enjoyable as eating popcorn. Perla had many questions in her mind about spiritual things; she had already taken The Bible School of the Air in Manila, and received her certificate of completion. One of Perla's questions was why should a person need to say prayers. Why shouldn't we be able to talk to God just like a friend? The Lord had His hand upon Perla long before we ever knew her and was even yet to show her His Glory.

While still in the hospital, I must have had a very high fever. Mrs. Labrador came over to my bedside, she turned over my very wet pillow. This was to be my very first encounter with the gentle, sweet nature of the Filipino people.

When it was certain we would be boarding the ship Johannesburg for Oriental shores, the students in Mrs. Peterson's Core class began saying, "Kay, perhaps you'll marry a Filipino." If not marriage, certainly there was to become a lasting bond between us and our Filipino Christian believers in such a way which only eternity will tell.

There are sometimes sacrifices that must be made in order for a missionary family to answer the call of the Lord upon their lives. Some of these sacrifices need to be made by the missionaries' children (the MK's) themselves. One of these sacrifices, which I was called upon to make, was having to say goodbye to our dog, Spot. For about five or six years Spot had been a very close companion to me. She was always at the back gate waiting for me to come home from school. She was always good-natured and would let me rough house with her. Biting at the water hose and playing tug of war was her endless delight. She would even sit up for me 'til the count of ten. One day at school, Mrs. Brown found me in the cloak closet. I told her although I was very thankful for the privilege to be going with my parents to the mission field, I was certainly going to miss our faithful dog, Spot. Mrs. Brown told me she understood how difficult it must be to be making the kind of change we as a family were being called upon to make. Many times our Lord will put us through a test to see if we love Him more than all these temporal things, which at the time seem so difficult to give up. The Lord had just the right place for Spot. As I shared before, Spot went to live with Aunt Katie, Uncle Harry and their two terrific kids, Margaret Ann and Harry. Spot would also be with Nicki, her very own puppy. Our Lord many times gives back to us those things we are willing to give up for the cause of His service.

Our final days in the States dwindled down to a precious few. The Lord even had just the right people to occupy our house. They were the brother and sister-in-law of friends of ours at Temple Baptist church. They took just as good care of our home as if we had continued to live in it. Family and friends did an excellent job of wishing us bon voyage, after all the packing for shipment and other responsibilities, twenty-one days crossing the Pacific ocean seemed to be a welcomed vacation. Little did we realize that we were in for a big surprise.

There was one more visit to Dr. Jacques at which time the brace was taken off my right leg. Dr. Jacques also reported to us that my physical therapy, which had continued for fifteen years, would no longer be necessary. Although there was no celebration or horn blowing because of this accomplishment, it was celebration enough for me that we were on our way out to the Philippine Islands. Dr. Jacques seemed to be very happy to hear of my parents' decision to accept another term of missionary service. Dr. Jacques even seemed to think the tropical climate would be good to relax my muscles.

BON VOYAGE

We moved out of our home a few weeks earlier than our sailing date, which was June 26, 1955, to give our renters the advantage of settling in. We stayed the rest of the time in a motel. Grandma gave us a farewell party. The whole family was there, so it seemed. This was the first time I had ever seen Grandpa in Grandma's apartment. Unbeknownst to us, we were seeing Grandpa for the last time on this earth.

The City of Johannesburg wasn't scheduled to leave the Long Beach harbor until the following morning. Family and friends  were welcomed to come on board ship and stay as long as they wanted. Everyone seemed to be accounted for but where was Grandpa? We knew he was staying with my Aunt Agnes. Did someone forget to pick him up? Mother jokingly said, "Perhaps Grandpa didn't want to be seen crying in front of all these church people." I'm sure there were many people there to say goodbye whom we wouldn't have missed at all, but Grandpa was a very important person.

En-route to San Francisco my multi-cultural education had already begun. The City of Johannesburg was a British ship with an Indian crew. My parents felt it to be the better part of wisdom for me to sleep in the double cabin with mother. Dad took the single cabin that was supposed to have been for me. Our cabin porter was a man from Calcutta. We told him about the FEBC. He promised he would try to listen on short wave radio when he got home. People in third world countries will have a short wave radio by their side if they don't have anything else.

In San Francisco we were allowed to get off the boat for the day. Dad's Aunt Bertha and cousin Bernice came into San Francisco from where they lived in Lodi to take us shopping. Dad needed to get some white shoes and white trousers, a wardrobe suitable for wearing in a tropical climate. Dad had lived with his aunt and cousin as a child growing up during the time his Father was a Chaplain in the Army during World War I. Aunt Bertha and her daughter had a wonderful conversion to Christ in the earlier years and expressed their happiness to have a part in our going out to the mission field once again.

The next morning we were on deck early to watch ourselves pull out of San Francisco harbor. The California sun did a silhouetted dance for us on the water. Dad reminded us of how many times we had driven across the Golden Gate Bridge. Now we were about to experience the awesome sensation of going under it.

Several days out at sea we had another new sensational experience, known by those who travel the high seas, crossing the International Date Line. We went to bed on Friday night and woke up on Sunday morning. We had lost a whole day. Dad didn't even have to mow the lawn. One day as dad and I were leaning over the starboard side of the ship watching the waves come crashing up against the hull of the boat, I happened to mention to dad that my arm felt so sticky. Dad informed me that we were now in tropical waters. Because of the high humidity, we would continue to feel very sticky for the full range of our missionary term.

The average missionary term is four years. Because of the added responsibility of the Director's family, the term is only two years. By this time we had come midway between the Golden Gate Bridge and Manila Bay. The captain asked my dad if he would like to visit the pilothouse. My dad considered the invitation an honor; he said, "Sure, I'd be delighted."

While being taken on this tour, dad was able to read the nautical maps. He saw the pinpoints showing a typhoon to the starboard side of us and another typhoon to the port side of us, the biggest typhoon of all was directly in front of us. My dad also observed that our ship had no radar. Of course we weren't the only passengers aboard ship, among the others was a missionary family of whom my dad felt a personal responsibility. They had a little boy, Richard about four years old and a baby in the crib. One day, Richard was discovered to be missing. Everyone searched the ship high and low. He was finally found down in the hull of the ship in the boiler room.

My dad let the captain know of his knowledge that we were in danger because of having no radar. He also told the captain of his knowing our situation in regards to the three typhoons, the most severe one of all being right in front of us. The captain seemed to be shocked that a missionary could be so smart. The evening of the very night we were to enter the heart of the typhoon was the captain's birthday. Everyone was invited but the missionary families decided to go to bed early.

We could hear loud celebration going on at the other end of the corridor. The captain was drunk. For some reason, dad decided not to go to bed but to stay awake and to leave the door of his cabin open. He was able to see and hear everything. Just a few feet away from where my dad was standing in his cabin doorway he saw the Captain of the ship slap the Chief Petty Officer. The captain saw my dad standing in the doorway. "Mr. Bronson, he said, I thought you went to bed. What did you see?" Dad told him he saw and heard everything, even the bad language. The Captain noticed my dad had everything recorded on paper. There wasn't much sleeping that night. What my dad predicted to happen actually did happen. The torrential rains, violet winds, waves as high as a ten story building, so it seemed, tossed the Johannesburg around like a matchstick. It was all we could do just to hold ourselves in bed. Mother and I could hear the ship's crew outside our portholes, frantically putting up the steel plates. When we first heard of not having any radar, perhaps we could have wished for the Johannesburg to turn around and head back for the Golden Gate Bridge if it hadn't been for the call of the Lord upon our lives. I always felt safe as long as I could be with mother and dad, whether it is on land or sea. My parents had their trust in the living Lord who promised to always take care of us. "The name of the Lord is a strong tower; the righteous run into it and is safe." Proverbs 18:10.

Getting up the next morning, we were greeted by a puddle of water that had lodged itself in the little hallway between the sleeping area of our cabin and the outside door, our lavatory was just to the right of the puddle. Fortunately, the Johannesburg was designed with typhoons in mind. Going down the corridor to breakfast the ship was still rocking like a cradle. We made practical use of railings on both sides of the corridors. A smile crossed my face as I remembered my physical therapist and Miss Williams telling me I walked like a sailor on board ship. Right then I was receiving first hand knowledge of what she meant.

In the dining room, or mess hall, as they sometimes call it, the sidings were put up on all four sides of the tables to make sure the food we were eating went inside our mouths instead of sliding off onto the floor.

After breakfast, the Captain wanted to see my dad in his private quarters. By this time the Captain was sober enough to feel remorse for all the happenings of the night before. He told my dad this was his last voyage before retirement. "Mr. Bronson, the Captain said, "if you report me right now, I'll be dishonored by the British ship lines and denied all of my retirement benefits." Dad reassured the Captain he wouldn't report him under one condition, that the Captain wouldn't make things go hard for the purser who had several years yet to go before his retirement.

Only then would all things be forgiven and whatever was recorded by my dad would be torn up and thrown into the waste paper basket. We'll never know if the Captain kept his promise but my dad certainly kept his with the satisfaction he was able to give the ole' captain a real good scare.

MANILA

The Johannesburg let down its anchors just outside Manila Bay, before being allowed to enter the harbor at which time the Filipino immigration officials came on board the ship. I remember my parents having to fill out and sign many papers and our American dollars were exchanged for pesos. One missionary once said to another missionary, "This peso money seems to be just like play money to me." The other missionary retorted back to her, "Ya, that's the way my wife spends it, just as if it were play money." Because of the seriousness of missionary life, many times missionaries learn to cultivate a sense of humor even if they don't really have one.

After being allowed to enter Manila harbor, our ship came to its final resting place. Leaning against the side of the ship, I saw those little brown faces hurrying about and speaking a language that was foreign to me, performing their daily routine just as their countrymen had done for centuries before them. I quickly had to readjust my thinking to realize this was the land of the brown face not the white face. This is a country they hold dear. We were the foreigners. Because of my CP, I wondered to myself if the Filipino people would not only look at me as a foreigner but as something from another planet. However, just as we were shortly to discover, there were many thousands of CP children in the Philippines. During our stay in Manila, we were to see only the beginning of anything at all being done to help them. As I sit here at my electronic typewriter reminiscing about our days spent in the Philippines, of which I'll never forget, I can't think of anytime in my life when I've received more love and understanding than I've received from our precious Filipino Christian believers.

All the missionaries from Christian Radio City were allowed to come on board ship to say, "MBOOHAY" (Welcome.) I noticed the backs of all the dresses and blouses of our lady missionaries seemed to be wet with perspiration. I made mention of it to one of the ladies and she just laughed and said, "We just get to where we don't worry about it, knowing we'll dry out later, such is life in a tropical climate."

It seemed wonderful to all three of us to step out onto dry land after twenty-one days crossing the great, seemingly endless, blue Pacific.

The drive home to CRCM was an experience I shall never forget as long as I live. We had to go through the very heart of the city in order to arrive at our little village of Carrohatten Pollo Bulacan. For the very first time in my life, my eyes were seeing poverty the way I had never seen it before. We had already seen the sunken Japanese ships in Manila Bay, with half of their hulls and masts sticking up out of the water to realize the Philippines was still suffering the devastation of war. Bob Pierce, founder and president of World Vision, once said in one of his many books before going home to be with Jesus, "No one has the right to call themselves a missionary until their heart has been broken over those things which break the heart of God." I saw precious little children floating little home made sailboats down the open sewers of Manila, which was their only playground. Mother had a difficult time getting used to seeing little children with open sores on their legs and not enough food to eat. The Filipino people may be very poor but they still know how to smile. I realize we have our very poor here in the States, but somehow in America there is still hope in even the poorest that perhaps someday they can rise above their circumstances. However, in those third world countries there is very little or no hope at all of a better life. Still, Manila is called the Pearl of the Orient because of its architectural style and culture. It's been my privilege to observe that our Christian nationals begin to gravitate to a higher standard of living because our Lord has promised to take care of his children. In Christ these people are given a future and a blessed hope. The very best missionary is a Christian national. In Manila we saw people living in squatter like conditions; homes made of cardboard, tin or whatever else they might find to give them shelter. This was a complete shock to a person like me who had always had all my needs and wants satisfied. In Manila, there is what is called the Walled City. Even there, families were actually living in bombed out holes in the walls.

Driving into CRCM's twelve acre compound, seemed like a little oasis or park with many trees and green grass. It's almost as if it was like heaven where everybody you meet is a Christian. However, missionaries still have a carnal nature as well as a spiritual nature. The only difference being the Lord's call upon their lives to go and do the job they're called upon to do. This is why missionaries need our prayers so they will remain faithful to the task the Lord has called them to do in a land where the culture is so much different than their own.

The first week of our stay in the Philippines, as I remember it, was mainly filled with getting settled in our little two-story Quonset Hut apartment where several other Directors' families had lived before us. During the first week, each missionary family took their turn to have the new Director's family in their home for dinner. It was very nice getting to know each missionary and their children. On a compound like ours, there were many children; American, American-British, American-Australian and many Filipino. The first evening of our arrival at CRCM, the missionary staff took us back into Manila for a Chinese dinner. Manila has a very large Chinatown. In fact the history books tell us the Chinese people were in the Philippines long before the Filipinos, themselves. The Filipino is a combination of Spanish, Indonesian and Chinese. Just before leaving home to go with our missionary staff into Manila, we were discussing the possibility of getting in touch with Perla before mother and dad got too busy at the radio station. Perla, as you recall was the very special Filipino girl we knew in the States at the Orthopedic Hospital in Los Angeles. In a city the size of Manila, it would take quite a search to find a person we had known a very short time under unusual circumstances. In the hurry of the moment such a thought was quickly erased from our minds.

The drive back to Manila was an eye opening and mind-boggling experience for all three of us, once again. All the sights, sounds and smells were far beyond anything we could have imagined. We couldn't have been there more than five or ten minutes with everyone talking at once, so it seemed, before noticing a lovely young lady entering the restaurant. She was in a wheelchair. My parents and I hadn't taken the time to ask the Lord for a miracle but there she was, Perla Labrador. Someone has perfectly stated, "In the Sovereignty of God, there isn't such a thing as a coincidence, but only a miracle." Through the directive hand of our Lord, we became close friends with Perla and her family.

After dinner, one of the missionaries put us on a calsa (horse and buggy). A calsa is only to carry people, a cartella carries produce to market. It's a horse with cart. It's very interesting to see the calsa and cartella going down the middle of the highway along with the natural flow of traffic. Along with the honking of horns and the policeman's whistle can also be heard the clip clop of horse hooves. To me Manila traffic was always more interesting than going to a three ringed circus in the States. Wherever there would be an officer of the law, there always seemed to be a traffic jam. One missionary described driving in Manila traffic: one foot on the gas, the other foot on the horn. Manila traffic might have seemed like a three-ringed circus to me, but I'm sure it was more of a headache to my dad who had to drive in it almost everyday. Mother completely refused to drive at all, content to be a missionary at the radio station, DZAS.

Our first night in the Philippines proved to be another new experience of sleeping under mosquito nets. The sheets were quite damp from the high humidity. I remembered seeing movies on television of men on African safaris. It was hard not to make the same comparison between them and us. Nevertheless, it was necessary to get a good night sleep; the next day would be immigration day. We couldn't really consider ourselves officially in the Philippines until the day ahead of us was behind us. To our way of thinking, there wasn't any reason to suspect immigration day to be more than routine, as it had been for every missionary family before us. Certainly it never entered our minds that my CP would be brought into question. Fortunately, our Brother Lacanilao became an angel unaware to us as he interceded for us before the top immigration official in Togalog, the national language of the Philippines. Although I wasn't able to understand the language at all, I knew Brother Lacanilao was pouring his heart out to his fellow countrymen on our behalf. It was a very touching thing to see. I tried to imagine what Brother Lacanilao was saying to this officer who to me looked more like a KGB agent. Unlike other Filipinos, who are very short with heavy black hair, this officer was a very tall man with absolutely no hair at all. I thought perhaps our Brother Lacanilao was giving reassurance to the official that my CP was only an injury from birth and not some dreaded disease we were bringing into the country. Perhaps he was also telling the officer about the FEBC and how it was a bulwark against communism in the free world. Brother Lacanilao was a Philippine national evangelist going on foot from barrio to barrio telling his own people about the Lord Jesus Christ. He has now gone to be with the Lord and Savior he loved and served. Whenever I think of him, it puts me in mind of the scripture which says, "How lovely on the mountains are the feet of him who brings good news, who announces peace and brings good news of happiness, who announces salvation and says to Zion, your God reigns." Isaiah 52:7 (NASB). For a short while, it was in question whether or not I would be allowed to stay in the Philippines because of my CP. Deep down in the secret corners of my heart, somehow, I was hoping they would send me home to the States. Manila, Philippines was still a very strange place to me. The only reasons I had for feeling at home was mother, dad and Coca-Cola. The whole world, so it seems, knows all about Coca-Cola yet there are 'untold millions' still untold of the precious gospel story of how God sent His only begotten Son into the world to redeem all mankind unto eternal life, why His precious blood was shed on Calvary, how He has risen from the dead or of the good news that He's coming back again, as King of Kings and Lord of Lords. Missionaries who I had never met before suddenly became my aunt and uncle.

Because of the tropical heat and very high humidity, which completely drained our energy, I also felt a siesta was a very good idea. The only time my dad didn't seem to think siesta was such a good idea is when he'd be right down in the heart of Manila, just about noon time, when all the government offices, shops, and restaurants would be closed for two hours lunch and siesta. The water in Manila was unfit to drink. Fortunately at CRCM, we had our own well and the water was very good. The Lord performed another miracle for us and we were given the privilege to stay in the PI (Philippine Islands).

The Lacanilao family became dear friends. Gloria, Brother Lacanilao's daughter, was a very dear friend to me all during our stay in the PI, a real sister in the Lord.

Although in the deep reservations of my heart there were feelings of being homesick and almost a delight in the Immigration officials wanting to send me home, yet the thought of being sent home without my parents would indeed be enough to horrify. On the other hand, if the Lord had really sent my parents to the Philippines to accomplish a mission for Him, certainly I would never want to stand in the way. After all, hadn't the Lord worked in my heart so as to give me the desire to be a missionary, too?

One morning we awoke to find mother very sick. She had been very sick all during the night. Mother called me to her bedside. Mother had always confided in me as a person far beyond my years. "Kay," mom asked, "do you think we're truly in the will of the Lord to be here in the Philippines?" I knew mother was too sick to fully comprehend what she was saying. She was also watching me become weaker every day from the extreme tropical climate. If Dr. Jacques ever thought the tropical weather would be good to relax my muscles, I'm sure he wasn't thinking about this. It just seemed as though the enemy (Satan) was attacking us on every front. Mother had to be rushed to the American Hospital in downtown Manila with a tropical infestation that was eating away at the lining of her stomach as well as consuming all the natural B vitamins, including Vitamin B12. It was hard to understand what could have made mother so ill so soon after our arrival in the PI. Dad quickly remembered that while the Johannesburg was still in the San Francisco harbor, there was a labor strike and the food which was to feed us while crossing the ocean was allowed to sit out on the dock in the hot afternoon sun. Mother remembered eating some vegetables on board ship, Brussel sprouts to be exact, which were very tainted. After being in the Philippines about a year, we met an American man in a restaurant in downtown Manila, who also had been very sick on the Johannesburg. He was an international businessman, stationed for a time in Manila. Not being a missionary or claiming to be spiritual in any way, he said, "I can't hardly wait to get out of here."

After a week or ten days in the American Hospital, it seemed as though mother was none the better. The only real help mother got for her illness was at the Seventh Day Adventist Hospital. They seemed to take a more personal interest, as a ministry, in helping those like mother. Nevertheless, we know the Lord had a purpose in the time spent in the hospital where mother had the privilege of meeting Ed and Helen Spahr, founders of the Grace Christian High School and pastors of Grace Bible Church in Manila. For the most part, Uncle Ed and Aunt Helen's ministry was with Chinese students, although another ministry in which the Lord greatly used them was in visiting hospitals. On one of their mercy errands to a lady missionary who had been seriously burned when an old refrigerator exploded in her face, Aunt Helen also visited mother. She was able to see mother was very sick. Aunt Helen invited mother and I to spend a week or so with them in their very nice Chinese style home. Uncle Ed and

Helen had been missionaries in the Philippines for twenty-five years. During the time mother and I spent in the home of the Spahr's, dad was back at the radio station busily getting our Quonset Hut duplex apartment more livable, at least the upstairs, with the help of Eingyong, one of our national workers, and a dear brother in the Lord. When we arrived at CRCM, there was an air conditioner in the Director's office. Dad gladly made the sacrifice to take the air conditioner out of his office so we could have our bedrooms air conditioned upstairs. Eingyong closed all the windows and cut a hole in the ply board wall between my bedroom and my parent's bedroom. This meant we could even use a light blanket at night. I was given a small desk from one of the studios on which I was able to do my correspondence school work. Before leaving the States, even my electric typewriter had been packed for shipment.

One time, I can remember the tropical climate had taken such a toll on me, that mother was even tempted to let me discontinue my studies but somehow the Lord gave me the courage to continue. Having an air-conditioned bedroom in no way diminished the reality that we were still living in a tropical climate, although we no longer had to sleep under mosquito net. The downstairs was one very large room. Mother got the bright idea to buy a bamboo curtain to divide the kitchen off from the living room and dining room.

The missionaries would make jokes about our "going behind the bamboo curtain." Living on a missionary compound such as ours, we were all as one big happy family. Our front door was open to missionary staff and

Filipino alike. An official patrol guard was given to guard the property at night. The first morning coming down stairs to breakfast, our house girl was skating the floor with one half of a coconut shell. This is a thing I had never seen before but I noticed the coconut shell had given the linoleum a very high shine. Dad had a special ant table made for the kitchen area. An ant table is a table with all four legs standing in little cans of ant poison. Everything in the way of food, which can't be put in the refrigerator, must go in or on the ant table.

Once a week, mother would go with the other lady missionaries into Manila to the Keyapo market to buy fruits and vegetables. Across the street from the Keyapo market is the Keyapo church where the Black Christ is housed. Filipinos came from many kilometers around to bow down and worship the Black Christ. What a privilege it is for us to go and tell them of the living Christ who is able to wash away their sin. Getting back home from market all fruits and vegetables must soak for one half hour in Clorox then washed thoroughly with soap and water. The egg lady came out to the radio station once a week. Meat was much too tough to cut with a knife. I wanted to throw it up against the wall but thought I would put a hole in our wall that was only made of woven bamboo grass matting. While we were in the Philippines, we learned to like rice very much.

One evening as we were seated at the dining table with missionary guests who were visiting the radio station, there came a very strange knock at the door. It was a postman with a telegram from California. Dear, precious Grandpa had gone home to be with Jesus. This was a very sad time for all three of us especially mother as she felt we hadn't said a proper and final goodbye to Grandpa because of our hoping he would be coming to the Long Beach Harbor to say goodbye. Whether or not the divorce had been grandpa's fault or grandma's I never took sides but when we got the news that grandpa had gone to a much better place, I couldn't help feeling that I had been able to bring a little ray of sunshine into his very lonely life.

When the news came of grandpa's passing, mother was still very sick in bed. I wanted to be able to comfort her but felt so inadequate to do so. Fortunately, mother was able to find her renewed strength in the power of the Holy Spirit. It was while mother was still in bed, the Lord burdened mother's heart to go out into the barrios and visit our Filipino staff families. I honestly do feel our Lord used mother in this way to bring unity between our Filipino and American staff, helping our Filipino believers to feel just as much a part of FEBC Ministry as any foreign missionary. Through mother's inspiration from the Lord, we began to have two Bible studies each week in our home, one being in English, the other in Tagalog, the national language of the Philippines.

Just as the Lord had sent Marilyn Roberts to be my friend in the States, He also sent Gloria Lacanilao to me there at the radio station. Gloria's brother Mike was the very best radio announcer on DZAS. Mike had a very deep clear voice and could speak flawless English. Although Tagalog is the national language of the Philippines, English is spoken throughout Manila, especially by the young. Gloria began coming up to my bedroom every Saturday morning to spend the entire day with me. This very close fellowship with the Filipino people made it a heart breaking experience to say goodbye when it was time to go back home to the States. Come to think of it now, I'm sure Gloria was also enjoying my air-conditioned bedroom. One day Gloria and I were sitting on the bed together and Gloria put her dark brown arm close up beside my white arm. "Kay," she said, "why is your arm so white and my arm is so brown?" It shocked me at first that Gloria would make such a comparison. I told her about people back in the States who spend hours in the sun down at the beach hoping to get brown. Gloria's eyes opened wide as saucers. "Kay, did you ever do that?" "Yes, I'm sure I did", I told her, "because I would like to be brown just like you." Gloria began teaching me a little Tagalog. One day I said to Gloria, "E cow I magunda (you are beautiful)." It truly came from my heart because that's truly the way I felt about her. Gloria said, "Kay, love is blind, you only say that because you love me." It thrilled me to know that within the short time we had been in the Philippines I had been able to communicate to Gloria my sincere love.

Coming downstairs to breakfast one morning my eyes fell on the headlines of the morning newspaper dad had left on the breakfast table. "President Magsaysay killed in plane crash." This had thrown the Philippines into national mourning. President Magsaysay wasn't just any ordinary President, he had a special understanding for the common people since he had risen up from where they were. When the Philippines lost President Magsaysay, they lost a real friend. Our family also felt a personal loss because of our friendship with Perla. During the national month of mourning, Perla and her mother came out to the radio station to visit us all dressed in black with black veil, the national dress of mourning. As director of Manila's finest music and cultural station DZFE and DZAS, Dad had been given a personal invitation to travel on the same airplane with the President. Although we deeply felt the loss of Magsaysay, on the other hand, we rejoiced that the Lord had spared the life of our dad. The Lord had called us to the Philippines and He had a job for us to accomplish, especially our dad. Traveling at night the airplane had crashed into a mountain instead of being directed around it. The plane was also carrying passengers and baggage over the maximum capacity. We were very thankful for the privilege to comfort Perla and the Labrador family at a most difficult time.

Some of the highlights of our stay in the Philippines were our many visits to the National Orthopedic Hospital with one of our single lady missionaries, Aunt Gilberta whom I had grown to love very much. Aunt Gil wasn't only a very fine Program Director at radio station DZAS, but also had a real missionary heart toward the Filipino people. Sometimes this would be most difficult for our missionaries to do because of being so busy doing their assigned job at the radio station, but Aunt Gil always made that special effort. Many times we would be invited on Aunt Gil's once a week visits to the National Orthopedic Hospital. In the States, my visits to the orthopedic hospital was only to benefit me. Here, I was going to the National Orthopedic Hospital to minister unto others.

Aunt Gil considered my CP another opportunity to minister Jesus' love to the patients. It also helped me to realize once again the faithfulness of our Lord to a person like me and realize that He loves each one of these people just as much as He does me. Most of the time I would see two or three patients sleeping in one single bed. The hospital had one special ward for patients with Cerebral Palsy. When we visited the ward, the children were busily doing their schoolwork. Even though their skin color was different than mine, I could see by their movements and even by their smiles that they were Cerebral Palsy. I thought to myself, "Yup, this is part of my clan." It was very hard for me to accept the fact that a child would actually need to live inside the hospital just because they were Cerebral Palsy in order for them to get the proper care and nutrition. Just before we were to leave the Philippines to return to the States, we were given an invitation to attend the celebration for the new Elk's Cerebral Palsy Center in Manila, in connection with the National Orthopedic Hospital of the Philippines. It was hard to fight back the tears of joy in the knowledge that for the very first time in the history of the Philippines, Cerebral Palsy children would be given some kind of hope for the future.

As program director of DZAS, Auntie Gilberta called upstairs above the studios to her little apartment. "Kay, I've been considering the possibility of starting a radio program especially designed to reach the handicapped." Of course, this came as no real shock to me. I already knew of Aunt Gil's compassion to reach out to people with special needs. She asked me if I would like to be the one to name the program. I knew right away Aunt Gilberta, in a tangible way, was trying to help me be a real missionary. The name, "Up Stream," immediately came to mind, however, this name, "Up Stream," wasn't original to me. I had seen a film in the U.S. about a little girl with CP. We wrote someone in the United States asking if it would be all right for us to use the name, "Up Stream," with the thought in mind that anyone can float down stream, but it takes real courage and perseverance to make your way up. To whoever it may have concerned in the States, they wrote back and reassured us that the Philippines was so far from the U.S., it didn't matter what we used on the radio. This gave me a little twinge of feeling homesick.

The radio program was a cultural type program, instead of being religious, with a gospel message at the beginning, in the middle, or at the end. And, of course, it was called, "Up Stream".

FOOTPRINTS

"During your times of trial and
suffering, when you see only one
set of footprints in the sand,
It was then that I your Lord carried you."

Author unknown

This is just one of the little poems I would hear Mike Lacanilao give on station break, but is very similar to what would also be given on, "Up Stream." More and more it seemed as though the Lord was unfailing in showing me the reason why He had dealt with me in the hospital the way He did. At the radio station, Sundays and holidays seemed to be the busiest days of the week or year. My friend, Kay Kaufman, had the original idea of having

Sunday school on Saturday so we could be free to go to church with our parents on Sunday. We had from eight to ten little preschoolers and kindergarteners in our Saturday 'Sunday' School. Kay asked me if I would come and lead the children in their little Sunday School chorus. One Saturday when Kay was away with her parents, she left me in charge of giving the lesson, as well as leading the children in their chorus and memory scripture verses. This made me very nervous. In a tropical climate, it's very difficult for a person to conceal their nervousness when the perspiration is pouring down one's face. The children seemed to think I was doing all right but in my own heart I knew I was doing a terrible job. When the children would be extra good or memorize their scriptures well, we would reward them with a stick of American spearmint gum. The gum looked delicious even to us as their teachers as it was a treat which couldn't be found anywhere in Manila, but we saved it just to reward the children.

As Director of Christian Radio City, Manila, my dad considered it only right for us to visit all the Evangelical churches, since our missionary staff represented a wide spectrum of denominations. However, the church we attended most was Grace Bible Church where Uncle Ed Spahr was the pastor. It was so much fun to sometimes sit in back of the church and watch all the ladies' fans going at the same time. In the States a lady needs to carry her handbag and Bible, the only difference in the Philippines, is a lady certainly wouldn't be without her fan. More often than not, after church we would have some other missionary couple to take out for dinner and a Sunday drive. Sundays were also the day off for the house girls, too. Sometimes, when no one else but us was in the car, we would go pick up Perla Labrador to take her for a drive. Being in a wheelchair and only able to walk a few steps on crutches, Perla was more or less a shut in. She enjoyed so much being able to ride in the car. It was on one of these occasions that Perla said, "Mr. Bronson, you know my country even better than I do." Once on a ride, Perla saw a vendor coming down the road on a bicycle pulling a cart stacked with bird cages. Some cages had only one sparrow, the other cages had two. Perla asked my dad to please stop. She wanted to buy us a bird cage with two sparrows. The vendor wanted four pesos. Perla haggled with the vendor until he gave the two sparrows for two pesos. The very next day the first sparrow died and about two or three days later the second sparrow died. It reminded me of the passage of scripture that could have been used on the radio program, "Up Stream."

"Are not two sparrows sold for a cent? And yet not one of them will fall to the ground apart from the Father. But the very hairs of your head are all numbered. Therefore, do not fear; you are of more value than many sparrows. Matthew 10:29, 30, 31.

I let my mind wander back to the first morning after our arrival in Manila. My curiosity, as I remember, just got the better of me and I took a stroll around the circumference of the twelve acre compound. The ground was rocky and difficult for me to walk on and to make matters even worse, a big brown dog kept following me. He wanted me to continually pet him as if to say, "Please let me be your friend." Coming up around the pathway between our Quonset Hut and the studio building, Perceso Marcello was standing in front of the studio building as if he were waiting for me. "Hi, Kay," I was surprised that he already knew my name, "that's my dog," he said. "His name is Febco for FEBC. I'll give him to you. He likes you." During the war, Percesco had been a "huck" warrior fighting for his country against the communists. He heard the gospel of Christ on the radio and turned his life completely over the Savior. He went to Bible school and became an Evangelist to his own people. One day it was my privilege to hear Percesco preach, although I was unable to understand the language. I could feel the anointing of the Holy Spirit in Percesco's preaching. One day he demonstrated to us how he could flip-out a bollow knife as quickly as anyone could blink an eye. I thought to myself, 'I'm sure glad the Lord got hold of your life.'

To be honest about it, Febby liked me much more than I ever liked him but he stayed around our front door enjoying the shade of the Banyan tree and we fed him leftover rice. Febby was a rice dog, there was no doubt about it. For some reason, the Filipino kids never liked Febco. One day they threw a rock and hit Febby in the eye. This was just the beginning of the end for poor Febco. The eye became swollen and infected. Febby also had other problems such as fleas and ticks which ate away at his fur and left blotches of infected skin. It got to the point where Febby had to be taken away. We heard later that someone had Febby for dinner. If I were as hungry as some of those provincial people, I'm sure I would have eaten Febby myself. However the Creator in no way forgot the Filipino people when he gave them twenty-seven different varieties of bananas, papayas the size of watermelons, mangoes and star apples.

In obedience to our Lord's call upon mother's life as a missionary to the Philippines, mother went out every week into the barrios to visit the people in their little nepa huts just to show them Jesus' love in the power of the blessed Holy Spirit. While in the Philippines, all three of us learned that the love of Jesus is able to cross any language barrier.

The Filipinos are very hospitable; they always want to feed you and give you their very best. They have so little of this world's possessions yet they give so much. The doctor told mother she would continue to be sick as long as she went to visit the Filipinos in their homes, as we Americans aren't used to eating as the Filipinos do. Mother told the doctor she had to be obedient to what the Lord had placed upon heart. It was very important to mother and dad to make the Filipino staff at DZAS know they were equally necessary to the radio ministry as any foreign missionary. At one point in our missionary term in the Philippines, Dr. Robert Bowman came out to the Christian Radio City, entered our house and found mother in tears. "What's the matter, Marge?" he questioned. She said that it hurt her to see the Filipino Christian believers living in such poverty. These dear people are so sold out in their commitment to the Lord and his service. Wouldn't it be wonderful if every Christian in America felt their personal responsibility to the work of the Lord in just the same way. CORRUPTIBLE EARTH? INCORRUPTIBLE CROWN.

Many times prosperity and greed turns peoples' hearts away from the Lord, or, when there is no restraint on the self will, even our precious Filipino believers could very easily become caught up in this lifestyle, as the nature of the fallen race of mankind is the same everywhere.

Sitting in front of my electric typewriter, I gaze out the window realizing my thoughts have taken me back over the years. It's been nostalgic for me to reminisce upon the goodness of the Lord to give me so many wonderful friends with whom to share the pathway of life. As I reflect upon memories of those who have made an imprint on my life, our Filipino house girl, Sabing, remains as keenly in my thoughts as any other. When Sabing came to live with us, she had never worked for Americans before. Even making a bed was a new experience for her but Sabing was highly intelligent and she learned quickly. Sabing came to us from the province of Tarloc, seventy kilometers north of Manila. Her father was a poor farmer. Sabing worked most of her youth with the rest of her family in the rice paddies and sugar cane. Although Sabing was able to speak almost perfect English, I think she had a more difficult time understanding me than I did her. She seemed happy to be able to tell me she was able to help teach the other children. How fortunate as Americans to live in the land of equal opportunity where even the handicapped are given a chance to prove what they can do. In recent years, mother has been able to teach me a little cooking and house keeping, enough to give me the feeling of self-reliance, if I would ever need to care for myself. When my parents call me Sabing, I always consider it a real compliment.

CHRISTMAS IN JULY, A SPECIAL GIFT BESTOWED BY THE U.S. NAVY... AND GRANDMA WATKINS

About midway into our missionary experience in the Philippines, Grandma Watkins had been so faithful to write us almost every week. Mrs. Brown had written me a long friendly letter filling me in on all the happenings at Lathrop Junior High School, a whole ocean away. Nancy Isle, the girl who had been an angel of mercy to me in Mrs. Peterson's core class, had also written a letter. In class, Nancy had taken carbon paper and recorded my assignment questions right along with her own in order for me to keep up with the rest of the class as well. It was very touching to us that our loved ones and friends would remember us so far away.

One day it seemed to be just like any other morning, I was busy doing my correspondence school when I heard someone running up the stairs just outside my bedroom. Peeking his head around the door, dad said, "Uncle Johnny is here." Just about as quickly, he was gone. I could hardly believe my ears, yet I knew it wasn't an impossibility as Uncle Johnny was an officer in the US Navy. The US Navy ships come in and out of Subic Bay, about a four-hour drive from Manila. This didn't seem to discourage Uncle Johnny, however. Boarding a Philippine bus isn't quite the same as boarding a bus in Los Angeles. In the Philippines, you most often will share a ride with a Billy goat, a rooster and, of course, overcrowding. By the time Uncle Johnny reached his destination, his officer's uniform, by some miracle, was as clean and pressed as if he had never encountered the experience.

The American missionaries seemed delighted to have Uncle Johnny at the radio station for his weekend leave from the Navy ship. Just seeing him in his officer's uniform gave them the feeling of home. Even Sabing seemed to enjoy having Uncle Johnny stay with us. She had a broad smile on her face as she pressed his uniform just a little. Still fresh in the memories of most Filipinos was the promise of General MacArthur, when he promised to return. I gave my bed to Uncle Johnny and slept in my parents' bedroom on an old army cot. I was so thrilled to have Uncle Johnny with us I would have been willing to sleep on the floor, Filipino style. The following day we took him on a short trip to Tagaytay just about an hour's drive south of Manila. Along the highway can be seen palm trees reaching up to the sky with their tops blown off. The Philippines at one time was filled with sounds of birds, but since the Japanese American war, not any more. Tagaytay is higher than Manila overlooking beautiful Toal Lake that has another lake with another island, one of the wonders of the world. Toal Lake has a little island in the middle of it. Within that island is another lake with an island. No one seems to get the explanation completely right the first time. I'm still not sure I did. On our return trip going back through the heat of Manila, we stopped at the US Military cemetery where there are placed row upon row of white crosses in memory of United States servicemen who gave their lives for the freedom of the Philippines. Uncle Joe's name, another brother of mother and Uncle Johnny's, was found listed on the monument for servicemen missing. Uncle Joe went down with his ship off the coast of Salvo Island, Guadacanal, August 7, 1942, on the USS Astoria. Just before heading back to the radio station, we stopped to watch one of the beautiful nightly sunsets over Manila Bay. Sabing told me a little joke once about a Filipino tour guide who took an American vacationer to overlook Manila Bay. The tour guide pointed to Manila Bay and "Tubig" (the Tagalog word for water). The American said, very assured of himself, "Oh, just regular size." Uncle Johnny seemed to enjoy watching the sunset over Manila Bay as the fishermen in their outrigger canoes with an abundant catch of daily fish made their way back to shore.

The next day just before Uncle Johnny was to leave us, and head back to his ship, dad took him on a private tour of the radio station. Uncle Johnny said he didn't realize the Far East Broadcasting Co had such a large radio facility in the Philippines. He was especially amazed at the awesome 750-foot radio tower with its very large antenna farm. He also saw the transmitter building and studio building for both short wave and medium wave broadcasting the good news of salvation.

It was difficult for all of us to let Uncle Johnny return to his ship, particularly for mother, as she had been so very ill and all three felt as though we hadn't been able to say a real goodbye to Grandpa. Seeing Uncle Johnny was a shot in the arm for us all.

In the Philippines there are only two seasons of weather, Hot and Very Hot. To us living in the PI, having Christmas in July didn't seem much different at all than if it had been in December. Our home church in Fullerton had a December Christmas party for the Bronson Family. Although we were charter members of the Temple Baptist church, we weren't considered Conservative Baptist missionaries. It was very encouraging to have our church remember our family in this way. At the December 1956 Christmas party for the Bronson's, each of the beautifully wrapped gifts had to be unwrapped and prepared for shipment in heavy steal galvanized drums on "a slow boat to China" to the Philippines. This was the reason for us having Christmas in July. We felt so rich compared to our poor Filipino people. I'm sure there were more items of clothing in the two barrels than our house girl had seen in a lifetime. Before we left the PI, it was our privilege to give so many nice things to our Filipino families.

NEW YEARS

Once again we were delighted when our church in Inglewood, CA, sent out a ham dinner for all the American missionary staff to celebrate New Year's Day. I'll long remember seeing the dinner table spread the full length of our dining and living room area. It reminded me of the Marriage Supper of the Lamb where all of us redeemed children of the Lord will share together in our heavenly home.

Instead of staying for the New Year's dinner, Kay Kaufman and I went into downtown Manila, to a teenage New Year's party given for the 25 American missionary kids of various mission organizations. We kids sure knew how to have a good time on a shoestring. We had a wonderful time that New Year's night, as I recall. Mother told me later there wasn't any room for us two girls at the banquet table anyway.

Actually Christmas and New Years are two grand celebrations in the PI. Our New Year's party continued until after midnight at which time we had to remain inside the house as it seemed too dangerous to even start back home. The Filipino kids were setting off so many firecrackers the entire atmosphere of Manila was filled with smoke. It seemed as if the Japanese had returned to Manila Bay. In those early days of missionary endeavor in the PI, besides our correspondence school assignments, the monthly teenage parties were just about all we kids had for recreation. Faith Academy for missionary children was still only a possibility being considered by a board of missionary parents. At this point in time, it's difficult to picture Manila as a Metropolitan city with high rise buildings, several television stations and even recreational areas. For a short time after we had come home to the states, it seemed as though our Filipinos were seeing days of prosperity that encouraged all of us so much.

For the most part, all the missionary kids were in harmony with what their parents were doing in the Philippines. In fact, many missionary children grow up to become missionaries themselves. There was only one teenager in Manila as I recall who seemed to have his mind set to the contrary. One day for some reason he seemed to have felt the need to confide in me. "Kay," he said, "it's hard for me to understand why we have to be here in the Philippines when we have such a beautiful country of our own." He expressed to me how he missed not having snow at Christmas. As I listened to him talk to me I was so deeply grateful to the Lord for the way in which He dealt with my rebellious heart during my stay in the Orthopedic Hospital of Los Angeles. I didn't want to come across to him with a "better than thou" attitude yet desired only to have my joy in the Lord's service come across. The one thing that helped me was the faithfulness of my parents to keep me close to them. Because of this, I will always have good memories of the PI.

When my parents first became involved with the FEBC, they were very much encouraged by the possibility of broadcasting into Russia. In 1939, the year of my birth, mother and dad were with the Russian and Eastern European Mission. The mission at that time had an orphanage, a Bible school and a church. Dad was working in the administrative office in the city of Danzig. Here my parents learned to know and love so many of the Russian and Slovakian believers who had suffered willingly for their faith in Christ. How wonderful was the vision of someday reaching their countrymen with the gospel of the Lord, by means of short wave radio that was able to penetrate any curtain. One day as I was walking around the compound at DZAS, Christian Radio City, the ground surrounding our duplex was very rocky, even the grassy area which looked so beautiful on the first day, I found out later to be full of potholes.

After surgery on my right foot, we had no way of knowing it would give us any further trouble. The Orthopedic Hospital in LA had been completely forgotten, the only memory we had chosen to keep was of our good friend, Perla Labrador. Why I had to sprain my foot and ankle bringing unwanted memories, I'll never know. We still believe everything that happens to us must be in the plan and purpose of our great God. It was necessary to take me to the hospital there in Manila. After being taken care of at the hospital and heading out Highway 54, we decided to stop at the airport to rest, it was such a hot and sultry day; mother wanted a cup of coffee. Dad said that coffee is too expensive at the airport but being the tender-hearted person dad always was, the final decision was to stop at the airport anyway. I stayed in the car with a splint on my leg and foot that would remain on for ten days. As mom and dad entered the coffee shop, they noticed the room was filled with European visitors. My parents had learned to speak German very well. Dad said to mother, "No, they're not speaking German, they're speaking Russian." My dad tried to count to ten in Russian, it got a smile but didn't make much of an impact. Finally, just as the people were getting ready to leave to return to their plane, my dad thought of one more word in Russian, "Slovabosha." which means, "Praise God." The young man jumped to his feet; pointing his finger to the sky, he shouted, "Slovabosha." Pointing to himself, he said, "I also, I also." What a time of rejoicing it was for my parents and those precious people to realize they were believers together in Christ. The younger man came over to where my dad stood, and said, "My grandfather would like for me to ask you a few questions. "Are you from a Christian radio station here in Manila," and gave the call letters on the short wave meter band. "Yes, we are," dad said. "Then, my friend, we have been listening to your station for many years." My parents brought them out to the car to meet me. One of the ladies gave me a Russian stamp for my stamp book. In all the excitement, they almost missed their plane to Australia, where they would live their new life in freedom. As they were hurrying to meet their plane, the man shouted back to my dad, "KEEP BROADCASTING IN THE RUSSIAN LANGUAGE." On the way back out to the radio station, dad told mother and I, "You know, we were receiving so few letters out of Russia, I had almost decided to take the

Russian programs off the air." Sometimes our Lord can even use a sprained ankle or a cup of coffee.

Throughout the 47 years of missionary service, my dad has often been engaged in diplomatic work on behalf of gospel missions. This displayed itself in a large degree in Manila. Dad along with his faithful companion, Max Atienza, negotiated for many months to get a bill passed through the Philippine congress to let all charitable organizations bring heavy equipment into the country free of tax and duty. Because of our friendship with Perla, we were given the right to take a tour of Malicanyeon, the White House of the Philippines.

On the last night of the congressional hearings, dad asked me if I would like to go and listen to the congressmen argue their lives away. I said without any hesitation, "Yes." I suggested we invite Kay Kaufman to go with us. Kay K. had been such a sweet friend to me. I appreciated so very much her being willing to share her Saturday, Sunday school with me. The House of Representatives was a smoke filled room which seemed to be an uncontrolled free for all as the congressmen lobbied their points of view for two or three hours. The Speaker of the House leaned back in his chair, put his feet upon the desk as if the situation was out of his hands, pulled out a bolo knife as if he were going to take a few heads in battle. Instead he whacked off the end of his cigar just to add to the atmosphere of the room already blue with smoke. By some miracle, the House passed the Bill and a recess was called, but the long night was only half over. Now the Bill was sent to the Senate. We only had a ten-minute break to get ourselves a hot coke. I can never remember having a cold one in Manila but it was better than drinking the water. At CRCM, we had our own well water which was safe to drink. After a short recess we had to hurry upstairs to the Senate chamber where the congressional arguments continued until long after midnight.

Sitting at my electric typewriter in 1992, looking back over the years gone by, especially our two years spent in the Philippines, seems like only a dream that we were ever out there, yet so many experiences will forever linger in my thoughts. In the year of 1956, the Billy Graham crusade came to the PI. This will forever hold a place in my memories because of the privilege Aunt Helen Spahr; mother, Kay Kaufman and I had of singing in the one thousand-voice choir. Once again it gave Kay K. and I another opportunity to be together. We went every Monday night for one month to choir rehearsal; we sang in the alto section of the choir. It was great fun. The most difficult part of all was to sing the High C in the Hallelujah chorus. The lady instructor looked over at me once or twice; I tried not to look handicapped and she tried not to notice I was handicapped. We worked very hard on the Hallelujah chorus trying to get it just perfect. At the last minute, Dr. Graham called and wanted to know what we were going to sing. When he found out it was the Hallelujah chorus he said that it was too "show offish." "I want you to sing John Stainer's classic, God So Loved the World." Dr. Graham had always been a very humble man. This is why I believe the Lord has been able to trust Ruth and Billy Graham in the limelight. Popularity never changed their personality or their message. We went over the music a few times with Cliff Barrows just before the one night crusade in the Manila stadium. It was going to be all right. The Manila newspapers reported the crusade to be of the devil. The newspaper headlines said to stay away from Billy Graham crusade. When people are told not to do something, that's the very thing they do. The meeting was to start at seven thirty. By seven, the stadium was filled to capacity and hundreds more were standing outside the gates. In the States our family isn't considered to be anything very special at all as far as the Graham Crusades are concerned. Perhaps we would be sitting on the highest bleacher back in a corner somewhere that is, many times, a more preferred place to be. In the Philippines, however, because of dad being the Director of the Christian radio station, he had been invited to sit on the platform. Mother and I, of course, were in the choir. Many times it was difficult to keep the Filipinos from treating us as if we were someone special just because our skin was white. One time, Gloria Lacanilao and I were in a radio studio where there was only one chair. Gloria wanted me to take the chair and I told her that if she sat on the floor, I would sit on the floor. When people have been put down for so many years, it's our duty as Christians to help them take their rightful place as heirs of God and joint heirs with our Lord Jesus Christ.

CORRUPTIBLE   INCORRUPTIBLE
EARTH?   CROWN.

Billy Graham certainly was anointed of the Holy Spirit to preach that night, just as always, just the ideal message for the multitudes of human souls who gathered together on that sultry, hot night. He spoke on the reincarnation of

Christ, comparing our Lord's leaving his throne of Gloria, with that of a human being willing to enter the world of ants in order to suffer and die for those ants. This is what the Lord Jesus did for us and not us only, but He took upon Himself the sin of the whole world. He actually left his Incorruptible Crown on high to enter into this Corruptible Earth, so we, by His Grace and power might, someday leave the Corruptible Earth for an Incorruptible Crown reserved in heaven for us. The Manila stadium was so filled with people there wasn't any room at all for people to come forward as in other Billy Graham Crusades. People were seated on the grass clear up to the podium where Billy Graham was standing. People who wished to make open acknowledgement of their decision to follow Christ were asked to stand in place. It was a wonderful sight, something I should never forget.

Strolling along the central pathway of Christian Radio City, heading in the direction of the U shaped studio and control bungalow one quiet, restful Sunday afternoon, while I was sitting outside the front door in a lounge chair under the shade of the Banyan tree, came three of four house girls. They came to where I was sitting and gathered around my chair. Usually, when the house girls get together there's lots of giggling.

In their native Tagalog they seemed to be very serious, no giggling at all. In English they asked me to open my mouth so they could look down my throat. I'm the one who wanted to laugh but they remained very serious so I tried to use self-control. I knew they wanted to ask why I talked so funny. After all, the other Americans didn't talk that way. Without any effort at all, I could have explained to them all about Cerebral Palsy but they seemed certain they had been able to keep their curiosity a secret from me. I'm not laughing any more. Now I realize the love and concern that was shown to me on that day from a people who spoke a different language than I.

It's wonderful to stop and contemplate the glorious future that awaits those of us who are believers in the Lord. I know many CPs who are believers in our Lord who happily look forward to receiving their new bodies in heaven. I think about heaven and all the riches of God's glory, which are stored up for us. I also enjoy picturing myself surrounded by Oriental brothers and sisters in the Lord as we worship our blessed Savior together. This will truly be heaven to me.

As I've written before, during the seemingly earlier years, 1955 – 1957, from my perspective, there seemed to be very little or no areas of recreation in or around the city of Manila, not to be compared with that of the States. However, as I recall, there were a few things of interest, recreational and historical. Like the time we went on a recreational outing with chaplains, pastors and missionaries in the Manila area. We took a Navy boat to Corregidor Island from the US Cavite Naval Base. In 1956, Corregidor seemed to look about as it did when our soldiers and sailors suffered so much and were taken prisoner, then forced to undergo the infamous death march up the Bataan Peninsula to prison camps. Everyone was in a somber mood and few spoke as we toured the island and saw places where fellow Americans suffered and died. We took a packed lunch and we kids were able to do some swimming off the side of the boat. On June

22, 1968, the Pacific War Memorial was dedicated and turned over to the Philippine government on the Island of Corregidor.

A delightful experience was when the Harlem Globe Trotters came to Manila. Once again, we went to the stadium with others of our DZAS missionary staff. As the orchestra began to play the Star Spangled Banner, I just happened to look up into the face of the missionary sitting beside me as the tears began to trickle down her cheeks. I remembered the teenager who had asked me why we had to be here in the Philippines when we have such a beautiful country of our own. The tears of this missionary seemed to answer the question. Missionaries are among our very best Americans; it isn't easy to be so far away from home even with a special call of God upon one's life and missionaries get homesick, too. The comic routine of  the Globe Trotters was enjoyed by the Filipino people; by the end of the game there wasn't a score on either side but one thing which did score was the renewed friendship between the USA and PI.

Bagio City was high up into the mountain, 70 kilometers north of Manila, with cool fresh air away from the tropical heat and humidity of the low lands. It seemed to be wonderful, almost too good to be true. One year and a half had gone by since our arrival on Philippine soil. By this time we were completely integrated into missionary life, as it was there in Manila. The Lord had made it possible for a bill to pass through congress that would contribute to the welfare of all mission organizations. Radio ministry is a twenty-four hour a day job. Most often dad would be up until early hours of the morning helping station technicians and radio programmers with their problems. He also had his own World News broadcast, getting up about four in the morning to get the news off the teletype to rewrite it for his 6:00 a.m. broadcast. Even the other missionaries seemed glad to make the sacrifice to let us go for a short weekend up to Bagio. We stopped to visit Sabing's parents home in Turloc, just a little bamboo hut with thatched roof. We understood why Sabing was such a nice person when we met her parents. Sabing had become a very satisfactory house girl for us; she, in fact, had become a part of our family. I felt as though I had a sister. We arrived in Bagio City right about dusk. I remember the beautiful sunset. The Filipinos were used to exquisite sunsets. We stayed at the Pines Hotel and had hot and cold running water that was a real treat for us. In Manila we had only one kind of water – lukewarm. Even our Lord didn't like lukewarm; neither do I.

Mother and I enjoyed a hot bath that was a real luxury for us. During our stay in Bagio, we attended the International Christian Leadership Conference on Evangelism. This is where I learned to know believers from around the world. In the Hotel I had the privilege of meeting Bob Pierce, the founder of I.C.L. His daughter Sharon was with him. She was a good friend of Kay Kaufman's. I learned to know Sharon better when she came to visit Kay at the radio station. The Pierce family must have suffered a lot with their father gone so much. It seems Bob tried to make it up to Sharon but it was too late. I remember her as being such a sweet girl although I thought she was very quiet. It hurt me very deeply to learn Sharon had taken her own life. The closer we come to the rapture of the church, it seems we hear of more sorrows and troubles all around the world. If we don't learn to fall upon the Rock, Jesus, and allow ourselves to be broken we will break.

It almost frightens me as I look back on it now to think of myself as not having CP. If we as humans never had to suffer in anyway, how could we identify with our Lord Jesus Christ in his suffering? Philippians 3:10, says, "That I may know Him and the power of His resurrection and the fellowship of His sufferings being conformed to his death, in order that I may attain resurrection from the dead." Verse 11, New American Standard Bible (NAS)

These majestic mountains of the Philippines are home to the Igrot people. To the Filipino mentality these are ignorant and uncivilized people where a boy isn't considered a man until he has taken a human head in battle. Yet, even the lives of people such as these have changed because of listening to the gospel message by means of a portable radio which the people themselves call, "God's box." On the way down the mountain, we stopped to visit an Igrot woman weaving a gorgeous tapestry. She was also chewing beetle nut, a narcotic gum that stains the mouth and teeth an orange like red that displayed itself in her brilliant smile. On our journey back to Manila we saw many hillsides of beautiful rice terraces, fresh and green from the recent rainy season. One of the Seven Wonders of the World, these rice terraces represent the ingenuity of the Filipino people. As we made our way closer to Christian

Radio City, we came upon Hector of rice paddies. Hector and the people were harvesting their rice singing in rhythm.

"Planting rice is never fun, bent
from morn 'till set of sun.
Cannot set, can not stand, and
cannot rest for a little bit."

Author unknown

Sort of whistle while you work. It's a good idea.

There are many new things for missionaries to learn when entering a new culture. At the beginning of our term in the Philippines, we were letting gospels of John and other types of Christian literature fly out the window to the people. However, we learned in a hurry, it wasn't such a great idea. The farm workers would even run out into the highway to get the treasured reading material, they have a hunger and thirst for knowledge and will read anything even if it's in English, but especially if it's in their own national language, Tagalog. If we don't get to these people with the gospel of Christ they will also read Communist propaganda. Needless to say, we had to relinquish this activity for the safety of the people.

The tropical sun cut across my windowpane like a laser beam, waking me up. A Filipino voice over the loud speaker at the radio studio said, "Hallelujah." This was not to be just any other day. There wouldn't be any time for my correspondence studies this day. It was the eighth anniversary of the FEBC in the Philippines. People from all across the 7,000 beautiful islands of the Philippine archipelago came to thank the Lord for the radio ministry which brought new life and hope into their darkened lives through the light of the gospel, peace with God and the hope of eternal life with him. Complete villages and barrios had come to know Christ through listening to just one portable radio, called a PM, or, portable missionary.

Mother and I had special Philippine dresses made for the celebration. Mother designed the dresses but the Mastesa sleeves were traditional dating back to the Spanish occupation of the Philippines.

During this festive occasion, I met a young man who was half-American and half-Filipino. These people are called Mastesa just like the Mastesa sleeves on my dress. It seemed as though this delightful gentleman was looking straight through me as if hoping to find a part of himself. I have wished many times I could have put him in my pocket and brought him home with me. I realize now he had just as much right to be here as I do.

Out in front of the studio the temporary platform was made of bamboo, banana leaves and beautiful white Sompageeta, the national flower of the Philippines. The President of the Philippines was there to give an address. Polly Lago sang,

"What Shall I Give Thee, Master?"
"Jesus, my Lord and Savior,
Thou hast given all for me.
Not just a part or half of my heart,
I shall give all to Thee."

By Homer W. Grimes

Each barrio in the Philippines has its own special day of fiesta. Certainly the eighth anniversary of FEBC was our fiesta day. On such a day as this, a pig is roasted on an open spit; this is called lichen and is very delicious. Ponte was also one of my favorite Philippine dishes; very thin noodles with pork and shrimp. I can only think of one Philippine delicacy that almost turned my stomach; goat's milk, sugar and pinto beans. We had to be very careful not to offend the Filipino people. Every culture is proud of their ethnic food.

At this point in time we had been over a year and a half in the Philippines, nearing the time of our departure from Manila, yet not knowing how soon we would be called back to the states. Our hearts had become very much a part of the Filipino people. Just as in the states, our interests were not only in the gospel ministry but also in pioneer work for the physically handicapped and especially Cerebral Palsy children. For centuries the Philippines had been living in the dark ages as far as any knowledge of Cerebral Palsy is concerned. A Cerebral Palsy child born into a Filipino family living in a provincial barrio would be shut away, the shame of the family. It was so good for me as a handicapped person to have lived even a short time in a third world country and realize how truly fortunate I am to be an American, to live in the land of opportunity for all, including a mentally challenged or physically handicapped person. As we gathered together in celebration of the opening of the Elks Cerebral Palsy foundation, I had heard of hand-me-down clothes but never had I seen hand-me-down leg braces. These little children were wearing braces twice the size of their own legs but at least it was a beginning towards rehabilitation, education and a future life for them.

Throughout our almost two years of ministry in the PI, the Lord was continually showing me reasons He put the desire in my heart to be a missionary. The FEBC is much set apart from any other missionary organization for this simple reason. The programmer sitting in front of a microphone doesn't have the convenience of seeing the person they are speaking to. After many months and even years, this can become very discouraging except for mail from hundreds and thousands of listeners who write the station even though it might be difficult to buy a stamp or even risk their lives such as in Soviet Russia. All of us at this point in time are very thankful this part of the world is opening up. While missionaries are ministering to others, many times missionaries need someone to minister to them. This privilege was given to me in a weekly staff prayer meeting. One of our missionaries received word from the doctor he had some spots on his lung. The prayer request for this missionary was given to me. I asked the Lord to remember Bob Kellum's faithful and important work for the ministry and to touch him in a very special way. Several days later Bob came storming into our side of the duplex happily shouting, "Where's Kay, where's Kay." He told me x-rays had been taken and the spots on his lungs were completely gone. Bob's ministry has continued in many other parts of the world and the United States. Our Lord does answer prayer at a time when He alone will get the Glory.

For the most part during our stay in the Philippines, we were able to maintain our American lifestyle. Even the

Filipino people were in some ways ready to latch on to an easier way of living such as dress and modes of transportation. Yet at the same time it was our desire to keep our home in such a way so as to allow the poorest Filipino to feel welcome in our home. Manila it seems is the hub of missionary activity. From Manila, missionaries branch out into other parts of the Orient. Many times a good description of our house could have been that of Grand Central Station with missionaries coming and going at all times of the day or night. Such it is, much of the time in missionary life.

Shortly before our return to the States, we had the privilege of staying over night in a nipa hut but it wasn't just any nipa hut. It was the home of Max Atienza's parents and where he had grown up. The Atienza family, many years before our visit, had heard the gospel message through listening to a portable radio. We went with Max and Sahra's family to Taal Batangus, a little province on the other side of Taal Lake. To me it is another wonder of the world. The Atienza family welcomed us into their humble dwelling just as if we were part of their family and, of course, we did sense oneness with this family of the Lord.

Though years slipped by us and memories begin to fade into history, it seems as though only yesterday we were climbing up the little bamboo ladder. It was such a delightful experience for all three of us. The hospitality of these people was far beyond that of anything we could have desired of anyone in the States. It's said many times what those who have traveled abroad know to be a fact, "Those who have the very least of the world's material goods are known to give the very most". Those who have been privileged to live abroad know this to be true. The tourist will never know, and it seemed as though during our stay, the Americans stationed there didn't really care. All their spare time was taken up with counting the days until their time to return to the States. When a missionary is really called by the Lord to go to a certain people, this is what makes all the difference.

Looking back on the situation, as it was in the 1950's, I believe with all my heart that Mrs. Brown was right when she said that I would learn more from my stay in the Orient than I could ever receive from a textbook.

Just before bedtime, the Atienza family gathered for prayer, each one took their turn including us children. The prayer time was long and deeply sincere. Although most Filipinos speak English in and around the Manila area, it seems more meaningful for them to enter the presence of the Lord in their native Tagalog.

There was only one bed in the house. The bed was given to mother and me. The Filipinos always want to give their best. Grandma Atienza brought out a set of pillowcases. They were new, the only ones she had ever owned. Mother and I could see they were the only treasures, with embroidery on them. Mother said, "Oh no, Mrs. Atienza, we don't need to use your best." "Oh, yes," the very elderly lady said, "You must, I do this as unto the Lord because you are his servants." For mother and I this was our first experience sleeping on a bed without any mattress. I doubt very much if mother or I got any sleep that night. It seems the dog barked all night.

The Filipino Nipa hut, with thatched roof and made of bamboo, is made in such a way as to also house the pigs, chickens, rooster and the barking dog underneath its floor, which is also made of bamboo strips so as to be able to watch the animals down below. The basic diet of the Filipino people is rice and fish; but for breakfast the next morning, they had prepared special for us, roasted chicken and eggs, just before our return trip back to Manila. The years have distanced us from that little Nipa hut and our visit with the Atienza family, but the memories will always remain fresh.

My Nipa Hut

My Nipa hut is very small but in
gathering seeds it houses them all.

By Felipe Padilla de Leon

The national worker is still the very best missionary. This was true when we were in the Philippines; it's even truer today as governments become less open to the foreign missionary. Max Atienza had been educated in the US. My dad appreciated so much Max's wisdom and knowledge in regard to protocol with government leaders and especially in overcoming the language barrier. Max had a very beautiful and intelligent wife, Sahra, a faithful encouragement in his ministry, yet maintaining the true Filipina style and grace.

Nearing the end of our missionary term in the Philippines, Manila no longer seemed to be the strange place to me as it did the first day of arrival. In fact, for us to return home to the States, it would be necessary for us to leave our little home at Christian Radio City, Manila, where we had learned to know and love the missionary and Filipino staff members. I also had the privilege of meeting world-renowned Christian leaders such as Bob Pierce. Dr. Barnhouse had breakfast in our home. In many ways the Filipino slow, easygoing way of life had been beneficial to me as a handicapped person. Returning home again to the states meant re-entering the fast lane where so often high blood pressure and obesity accompany the good life.

DEPARTURE APPROACHING

The most difficult part about returning to the States for us was saying goodbye to our Filipino friends. If ever I was going to be spoiled, the Filipinos are the ones who did it. Whatever spoiling my parents had accomplished in the beginning, the Filipinos finished it off. Our family had to make a lot of changes during the earlier time but departing from Manila is one of the most difficult things I ever had  to do. I didn't realize at the time that many of our best Filipino Christian leaders with their families would be coming to live in the United States. Although we appreciate their desire for a better life here in the States, at the same time it saddens us to see the Philippines losing some of their finest National pastors and evangelists. Some of them, such as the Atienza family expressed their fears of Communism someday infiltrating the Philippines. Our earnest prayer is for the Philippines to remain open to the gospel message.

Since our return to the States, and down through the years we've heard many encouraging stories about the faithfulness of our Lord to His servants in the Philippines. Some distance away from the corruption and unrest of Metro Manila life, a nucleus of Christians who built their own little church of bamboo and a thatched roof, was meeting. As the national pastor got up one Sunday morning to deliver his sermon, he stopped right in the middle of it and said to his little congregation, "For some reason I feel the Lord would have us get down on our knees and pray." It was only a few seconds before the doors of the little church opened with Communists with bayonet machine guns shooting up the whole church. Fortunately, no one was injured because they were all down on their knees praying. I have often wondered what those dear Christian believers must have been praying about; if perhaps they were praying for us, then by all means shouldn't we be praying for them?

We as Christians are so fortunate in that we will always have something to do, because if we can't do anything else, we can pray. In prayer we can reach around the globe then touch the very heart of God. Through prayer we can pull down the strongholds of Satan and storm the floodgates of heaven. A person who is severely handicapped can actually rule the world through prayer.

"For though we walk in the flesh, we do not war according to the flesh, for the weapons of our warfare are not of the flesh, but divinely powerful for the destruction of fortresses. 2 Cor. 10:3, 4, CORRUPTIBLE EARTH? INCORRUPTIBLE CROWN.

As I've mentioned before, during the 60's and 70's, it seemed for a short time the Philippines was beginning to see the light at the end of a very long and dark tunnel, economically. The hopes and dreams of the Filipino people took an up swing. American nuclear plants invested industries in the Philippines. Filipinos left their sugar cane fields, which was their national export product, to work in the nuclear plants. As a result, their standard of living rose higher. The Filipinos were once again devastated when the American nuclear plants decided to move to a different location outside the PI. By this time the sugar cane fields had been left to ruin and the rug, as it were, was completely pulled out from under the Filipinos. In this national condition, with little children climbing around trash heaps trying to find a few morsels to eat, it's simple to understand how the unregenerate mind would be sucked into the lies of a Communist ideology. While stationed in the Philippines, my parents captured the vision of training the national Christian for leadership in the gospel ministry in the event of countries becoming closed to the white face and the foreign missionary.

Returning to the states meant I was certainly going to miss my Aunt Gilberta Walton. Gilberta was a single missionary. The Scriptures teach us the married person is concerned about how they may please their spouse and a single person is concerned about how they may please the Lord. Gilberta was a true example to me of a single person's desire to please the Lord. After Gil's responsibilities at the radio station were completed, instead of dwelling upon her own loneliness and feeling sorry for herself, she reached out into the surrounding barrios to minister unto others.

As I've mentioned before, Gilberta's faithful ministry at the National Orthopedic Hospital was an inspiration to me.

Without any previous knowledge of the promise that the Lord had given me in the Orthopedic Hospital of Los Angeles, Aunt Gilberta had been a part of its fulfillment; and the program "Up Stream" was developed. It must not have been more than just a year or more since our return to the States before Aunt Gilberta came home for a year of furlough. At a missionary conference in Burbank, California, it seemed the Lord turned the tables around just a little so were able to be a part of the Lord's intervention into Gilberta's life. He gave mother the privilege of introducing Gilberta to her future husband, a missionary to Liberia, Africa. After suffering the loss of his dear wife in Liberia, this man's dedication to missionary service met its equal in Gilberta. The Lord had rewarded Gilberta's faithful years to His service. Just as the Lord blessed Gilberta's ministry in the Philippines, she was also an instrument in the Master's Hands for many years in Liberia before He took Gilberta to her eternal reward.

Although our friendship with Perla Labrador had deepened through the few years of our stay in the PI and she had expressed openly to us her interest in spiritual things, still we weren't completely certain of Perla's full surrender of her life to the Lord. There were many conflicts within Perla's heart and mind. Like all of us, Perla wouldn't find peace or rest until she turned everything over to Him. Sometimes we think it's all up to us to get a person on the right track for the Lord, when in reality we need to step out of the way in order to allow the Lord to do His sovereign work. The Lord wanted to use other people in Perla's spiritual life and not just us.

We had decided a long time ago that ocean voyaging would never have the romantic spell on us that it might have had once. Dad promised mother and me when it came time for us to return to the States it would positively be by airplane. No more typhoons for us. I don't mind being called a missionary as long as we don't have to cross that ocean again. A little boy was once asked what he wanted to be when he grew up. He said, "I want to be a missionary home on furlough." We've been home on furlough for thirty-five years now and I still don't want to cross the ocean again, but I believe our experience in the Philippines has helped me be able to pray more effectively for our missionaries.

I firmly believe short term missionary service is a good idea because even if a young person decides on another career, their short term mission field experience will give them first hand knowledge of the world's need for the gospel of Christ.

The national staff of DZAS took us out to Max's Chicken for a farewell dinner. This isn't our very own Max Atienza, however. This is another Max who, also, was educated in the US, came back to the Philippines and made himself a fortune. Often times, Max would come and sit down at our table just to talk. My dad would try his best to get Max to divulge his secret recipe but he was too smart. He never would do it. This time we were given a private room for our dinner party. Dad, mother and I were each to give a farewell speech. Mom and dad did all right, when it came time for me to say something, I began to cry. My uncontrolled emotion was an embarrassment to me but I felt frustrated and didn't know what to do. Many times CP people have a difficult time controlling their emotion when they feel things deeply. The Filipinos had treated me like a little princess and this was one of those special occasions for me.

GRANDPA AND
GRANDMA BRONSON

The airlines gave us three options. We could return to the States by way of Europe, Hawaii or the Aleutian Island chain. The reason for our choice of the latter was for us to be able to visit Grandpa Bronson in Seattle, Washington.

Much to my regret, I never really felt close to Grandpa and Grandma Bronson, although I loved and admired them more than words can ever say. Most of my growing up years, the Bronson's were living in Seattle, Washington, where grandpa was a teacher and business administrator at Northwest Bible College. In the early days, Grandpa was a circuit riding preacher for the Methodist Church. My dad told us about grandpa pastoring five different churches on Sunday. He was also First Lieutenant, Chaplain, U.S. Army. In World War I, Grandpa and Grandma never owned their own home or even a car. They always lived in a parsonage. This present world held little known value to them. Grandpa patterned his life after the famous George Mueller, Englishman, founder and administrator of a large orphanage. They lived sacrificial lives. It's a shame we couldn't have lived closer to the Bronson's. I'm sure they would have had a great impact on my young life. By this time, Grandma had gone to be with the Lord after a battle for years with cancer. Grandpa was retired from the Northwest Bible College and all alone in a very small apartment.

The missionaries were out extra early to see us off at Manila International Airport. As soon as we took off, I knew for sure that aviation was in my blood. What's wrong with being on cloud nine? The only problem is that once in a while we have to come down. My love for the sky made me know I was my father's own child for sure. I remember dad telling me if I hadn't been handicapped, he gladly would have given me flying lessons. Dad remembers having the privilege of meeting Amelia Earhart during his years at Douglas Aircraft plant. My dad always seemed to admire a woman who could take to the sky. For a man to engage in some things was normal, but for a woman, that was something else.

AIRBORNE

After taking off from Manila International, it was hard to believe within just two and half-hours we would be touching ground in Hong Kong. Just a few months short of two years, Manila had been our whole world. Yet it seemed as though the Chinese in Hong Kong were going about their daily labors unaware of any existence outside of theirs. I've always been one to enjoy getting some place in a hurry. These planes are really wonderful. On the ship, Johannesburg, I felt we could have gone faster if we were to jump overboard and swim. The only problem is neither of us can swim that well. We arrived in Hong Kong about noon that day. One thing I observed was that they had daylight savings time. In Manila everything was pitch dark at 6:00 p.m., year round. In Hong Kong we had one whole afternoon, evening and another full day. The Airlines put us up in a hotel in Kowloon on the mainland of China. We then took the ferry over to Hong Kong. Our good friends, Rev. Ed and Helen Spahr, gave us money to have ourselves a good time in Hong Kong. We sure did.

People from around the world stop off in Hong Kong to shop. It's heart breaking to realize that in just a few years, freedom loving Hong Kong will be surrendered to the mainland (China). It was thrilling to see the Billy Graham Crusades from Hong Kong on television several years ago as Chinese people by the thousands responded to the claims of Christ. Hong Kong has heard the gospel message and they can still hear by short wave radio from the FEBC even though curtains may fall.

We crossed over on the ferry many times during our short stay in Hong Kong. As a little girl, my parents read stories to me about the early missionaries visiting the Chinese people on their san pans telling them about the love of Jesus. Now, I was actually seeing first hand how these people live on their very small boats, more often than not with a very large family. As our ferry eased into the harbor for the second time, I tried to look closer to see how the people were surviving on river homes. A person would need to be very calcite not to have their hearts go out to those people.

As I watched, a mother was boiling her large kettle of rice on the back end of possibly the only dwelling they had ever known, as the steam from the rice encircled a string of wet clothes hung out to dry. However, many have swam this same river to freedom in Hong Kong; freedom is precious to these people. It seemed to me as if everyone was walking about Hong Kong in his or her pajamas. As a teenager I must have wished I could do that. In Hong Kong, I noticed women were being forced to do backbreaking labor the same as men.

If the women's liberation movement in the United States desired equality with men, they should go to Hong Kong. It was hard for me, as I'm sure it was for my parents, to see human beings used like beasts of burden. I even felt sorry for the men who had to carry me in his rickshaw. Yet if we don't take their services, we deprive them of earning much needed money. The noonday sun seemed almost to be cruel as it shone down on these poor people, while shop owners made a fortune on the tourists. It was almost a welcomed relief to be up in the clouds once again. Yet I wondered if we had been called as missionaries to some parts of free China, such as Formosa, that was going to be our net stop, would I be able to love these people as much as I love the Filipinos. Certainly God does love them very much. Some of the most highly skilled and professional people are the Chinese. Even with all the intelligence and technical abilities of mankind, God looks down and only sees the heart.

On the island of Formosa, or Taiwan, the living conditions of the people seemed to be the same as Hong Kong except for the fact that Taiwan isn't the tourist trap as Hong Kong. The FEBC has radio studios on this island that at the time were under the direction of Richard Rowland.

We were scheduled for three days stay on Taiwan and had the privilege of living in the home of Mrs. Lillian Dickson. She was a long time missionary to China and wrote the book, "These My People". Mrs. Dickson is best known for her work with homeless children. During our stay with her, the hallways of their home were lined with baby cribs ready to be delivered to a nearby orphanage. Dick Rowland took us on a bus tour of the island. That same evening we were invited to have dinner with the Jim Grahams. We had the privilege of knowing Sophie Graham, Jim's sister, during our short stay in Manila. Two years is really only time enough to get to know and love people. Then another transition must be made, but God is even in our transitions and we can trust in Him. Sophie Graham was a well beloved Bible teacher in Manila. Dick Rowland also took us to visit the radio station of FEBC where Chinese programs are made by Chinese Christians for broadcasting back to mainland China from the FEBC short wave stations in Manila. While we were still visiting the radio studios on Formosa, we just happened to notice a very lovely lady at the organ.

Dick had been a single missionary for many years, first in Manila, then on the Island of Taiwan. Dick said, "Do you like the lady at the organ?" We all chimed together, "Yes we do." Dick did too and very soon after our arrival in the States, Dick and Mary Ellen married.

On our continued trip back to America, our next stop was Okinawa. Now at this time in my life if the Lord were to call me to be a missionary I would ask him never to send me to Okinawa. To be called to the Philippines would be like going back home again to see my friends, although so many of them are now in the States. On the other hand, if I were called to be a missionary in Hong Kong perhaps that would be all right although I would probably be shopping all the time. If the Lord were to send me to Taiwan as a missionary, I would wish I could be like Mrs. Lillian Dickson, a woman the world would disregard. Disregard as not having any outward beauty but who was lovely on the inside with a radiance that only comes from Christ. But, Lord, I would pray, NEVER send me to Okinawa. That would certainly be a true test of my calling. Doris and Jim Copel, missionaries with us at Christian Radio

City, Manila, were chosen and sent to Okinawa to start a local Christian radio station to reach US servicemen on the huge US Naval base there. We stayed four days with Jim, Doris and their little baby girl who had been born in Manila.

Okinawa is a very desolate island that was once occupied by the Japanese. The few people living on Okinawa are called Ryukians and are descendants of the Japanese. We had a wonderful time with Jim and Doris renewing our friendship. On the CRCM compound we had become as one family. If someone on the compound was baking a cake, everyone knew about it. I observed on Okinawa, the humidity was much higher than in Manila, as the sheets on our beds were actually wet from the dampness in the air. What a place to be called to be a missionary. Perhaps Manila seemed more like a heaven on earth to Doris and Jim after living on this inhospitable island, famous for its suicide cliff, better known as "Hack Saw Ridge," where people have been known to jump to their deaths during the war.

Our next destination was Tokyo, Japan. Now if it had been my responsibility to schedule our trip back to the States, I would have given us one day on Okinawa and four days in Tokyo. As it was, we were only given one day in Tokyo. No one asked my opinion; the airlines didn't even ask my parents. Yes, I've been to Tokyo, Japan, yet I feel I know nothing about it except for what I've learned from history. I've been to Hong Kong, Taiwan, Okinawa and Japan, yet I know absolutely nothing of any of these countries. No one is privileged to know any one certain country unless they've come to know the heart beat of its people.

Looking back, as the ship, Johannesburg, eased its way through the gates of Manila Bay, I wondered if the Filipinos would consider me not only as a foreigner but also as something from another planet because of my Cerebral Palsy. I've learned, however, over the years, every country has its handicapped children and adults. There are many thousand of Cerebral Palsy persons throughout the world. Many of these people are considered outcasts of society among their own people and not of any worth. Many of these individuals have been able to hear the life-changing message of Jesus Christ by means of short wave radio. Many of them for the first time in their lives are now able to sing, "No One Ever Cared for me Like Jesus." A letter was received from a blind man living in Japan who heard the gospel of Christ for the very first time through listening to the FEBC. He is now the pastor of a small congregation.

Our Lord didn't come to earth to die for nobodies. In Christ everyone is somebody. "For you once were not a people but now you are the people of God; you had not received mercy, but now you have received mercy." I Peter 2:10. "The first link between my soul and Christ is not my goodness but my badness, not my merit, but my misery, not my standing, but my failing, not my riches, but my need." Charles Spurgeon CORRUPTIBLE EARTH? INCORRUPTIBLE CROWN.

As our plane reduced its altitude for a touch down at Tokyo International Airport, mother told us later, "As I looked out the window of the plane, a deep seated anger that I didn't realize I had in myself, welled up inside of me." "These people killed my brother", mother said. She was shocked almost to the point of tears at the awareness of her own feelings. "Jesus, please forgive me." Through the years mother had struggled long to make me self-reliant. Now she was teaching me how to confess my sin of resentment and lack of trust in the sovereign Lord; also how to forgive. She continued to teach me this truth by her daily example of commitment to the authority of Christ. "Casting all your anxiety upon Him, because He cares for you." I Peter 5:7

Among the first shipload of FEBC missionaries to set foot on Philippine soil in 1946, were the Krepts family. As the years drifted by they became missionaries to Japan with the Conservative Baptist mission board. We were grateful to have them welcome us at the Tokyo International Airport. To my way of thinking, Tokyo resembled the nearest comparison to an American city I had seen in the Orient. This somewhat surprised me because I had read and seen from documentaries of history how Tokyo had been devastated many times by bombs and earthquakes. The city certainly revealed the competitive spirit of the Japanese people even in those earlier days.

It was so nice to have the Krepts come to meet us at the airport. They took us through the central part of Tokyo. Everything seemed very westernized except for the smells that seemed more like Manila. Someone has said, "In order to be a good missionary, sometimes you need a sanctified nose." The Krepts took us to their apartment that was very Japanese with an American touch. I fell in love with it. It looked as if they had been there a long time and were planning to stay even longer. The next morning the Krepts had breakfast with us at our hotel; we also did some shopping before returning to the airport. By this time we were beginning to feel more at home up in the air than down on the ground. After supper we were given pillows to bed down for the night.

There had been another exquisite sunset for us to behold; we had a heavenly view. Within just a few hours we saw the sunrise. Again we were back on the other side of the world.

Our next destination was the Aleutian Island chain, 1,100 miles stretched out across the sea. They looked like fallen asteroids dotting the coastline. Our plane made another touchdown on the little island of Shimia, Alaska. Even the name, Shimia leaves me cold. I hope we never have to be that cold again. Our blood must have been very thin from living in the tropics; fortunately, we were on the island for only one hour. The airport was the only thing on the island. We were escorted from the plane to just a shack of a waiting room. We were returning home in the summer, I guess we would have felt even colder if it had been winter. Dad made a telephone call to Grandpa Bronson in Seattle.

By this time, grandpa had been retired from Northwest Bible College for several years. He retired earlier than expected to be able to more lovingly and efficiently take care of grandma, who had suffered with cancer and diabetes. The diabetes had robbed her of her eyesight and cancer had eaten away at her intestines to where she was no longer able to eat. I loved my grandmother very much because of the blessing she had been to me during my spiritual struggles, accepting myself as a handicapped person. Grandma has gone to be with the Lord for her final and complete healing. Grandpa had been living alone for several years in a small one-bedroom apartment that still held memories of his beloved wife. It was to be a complete surprise to receive a phone call from a part of himself that he thought was still in the Philippines. We were hoping to not give a sweet old man a heart attack. We were able to spend a few days with Grandpa Bronson before reaching California and HOME. We were able to see just how beloved grandpa was among the Christian believers in the Seattle area. Some of them had us in their home for dinner; others took us to a restaurant. The most outstanding thing to me was all the white faces, no brown faces could I see anywhere. My white face blended in with all the other white faces and no one seemed to notice or even care that my heart was still Filipino.

Grandpa Bronson was a blessing to others for several more years before he was taken home to be with the Lord. After Grandpa Bronson's departure from this life, the Northwest Bible College named their new administration building, Bronson Hall. This could never have happened with grandpa still on this earth. Grandpa was a very humble servant of the Lord and didn't want to take any glory to himself.

HOME

On our trip down the coast to Southern California, it seems as though my thoughts were only of our dog. I remembered the Lord witnessing to my heart that if I would give Spot up for Him to go to the mission field for a short time, He would keep Spot for us. Yet it seemed almost wrong to even expect she would remember us after that length of time. When we went to visit the family Spot was living with she just looked at us as if to say, "Oh, are you back again?" She continued to play in the backyard with her adult offspring just as if to say, "These people have been treating me well, why should I be concerned about you?" I always did surmise that Spot could be fickle because she seemed to love everybody, but I guess I just under estimated her intelligence. We almost decided to go home without her. As we were all three settled in the car ready to go home, Spot jumped into the front seat positioning himself in between mom and dad as if to say, "I'm ready, let's go home." Now I knew for sure she was the smartest dog in the world.

Looking back upon those first few days after our return to the States, it's hard to understand how I could ever think time would just stand still and wait for us to get back. History has proven "time waits for no one." It seems so many changes had taken place in the States while we were gone. For one thing, my cousin, Margaret Ann, had gotten married. I thought for sure after Margaret Ann was married she would forget all about her cousin, Kay. It was a complete surprise to me when Margaret and her husband, Ray, expressed their desire to take me to Disneyland. Disneyland had opened up during the time we were in the Philippines. I hadn't seen it before. Looking back on it now in retrospect, I realize Margaret and Ray were helping me get readjusted to the white culture. While we were at Disneyland something very special happened. I met a missionary family I had known in Manila. It was a complete surprise to see the Honeywells at Disneyland. I didn't know it was their time for furlough. We had come to know them very well, as they were administration leaders at the Febias Bible Institute just adjacent to Christian Radio City. Their daughter, Carol, had been one of my teenage friends in Manila. I always admired Carol's commitment to the Lord and understanding of what her parents were doing in the Philippines. Over the many years of living there at Febias, Carol had learned to speak Tagalog. Since most Filipinos know English, it's a compliment to them when missionaries make an effort to learn their language. It was so nice to see them again within just a few weeks on the other side of the world. Truly, "IT'S A SMALL, SMALL WORLD."

It's been delightful down through the years not only to watch my close cousins grow up to be responsible adults, but also to raise families of their own and even become grandparents themselves. It's simply amazing to me how a modern day housewife can manage her family well and at the same time be a part of the outside work force. Down deep in my heart I think they must be a little crazy; yet at the same time they hold my highest admiration. I realize for a woman 'working out' might be necessary, but not always the best.

Just as women in childbirth, in some ways I feel as though I'm just about ready to give birth to this book. Birth pains have been very long and excruciating at times. I thought to myself, many times, if Margaret Ann can raise four kids at least I can write a book. Someone has said, "If you want to be a writer, write about something you know." By the time this book is finished, it will contain just about all I know. I told the Lord if He wanted this little piece of history to be written, it would need to be His story. I realize I could never see it to completion without the strength of the Lord and this new, Brother, word processor given to me by very dear friends, the Mooney family. At this point in my life, I've been attending Mary Ann Mooney's Bible study for about six years. Mary Ann is a graduate of Wheaton College in Illinois. My first electric typewriter was provided by my Uncle Bob Bronson, from his Douglas Air Craft plant here in Southern California. It was an old pre-war model which looked more like a battleship than a typewriter, but it opened a whole new world for me. Even if no one ever cared to read this life's account, it's been good for me to realize, once again, the faithfulness of our Lord. I'm not anyone special, our Lord is able to do this for any "handicapped" who will surrender their future into His hands. When I was just a child still in Washington Boulevard School, we had no idea I would ever be able to complete a sentence, or write a paragraph, or write a book. Miracles do happen, and the Lord has used many wonderful people to help accomplish it.

It was an old pre-war model, which looked more like a battleship than a typewriter, but it opened a whole new world for me. Even if no one ever cares to read this life's account it's been good for me to realize once again, the faithfulness of our Lord. I'm not anyone "special", our Lord is able to do this for any "handicapped" who will surrender their future into His hands. When I was just a child still in Washington Boulevard School, we had no idea I would ever be able to complete a sentence or write a paragraph, or write a book. Miracles do happen and the Lord has used many wonderful people to help accomplish it.

I continued to correspond with, Perla Labrador, 'till she went to be with our Lord. Perla, had a desire to know the Lord long before we ever knew her at the Orthopedic Hospital in Los Angeles, but family traditions and her complete dependence upon her family for even her simple every day needs hindered Perla, in many ways, from making her final commitment of her life to Christ. One day, Perla, called the radio station there in Manila. She needed someone to talk with her concerning her spiritual needs. Mike Lacanilao, talked with her on the phone for almost an hour; Perla prayed with Mike to receive the Lord Jesus into her heart as her personal Savior. Perla was determined to follow Christ even through much persecution. She wrote to me many times and expressed her love for the Lord.

The blessed Holy Spirit continued to work in Perla's life conforming her into Christ likeness. Shortly after Perla's decision to follow Christ, her parents sent her on a trip around the world with only a private nurse by her side. This showed their complete confidence in Perla's capabilities, but at the same time they were hoping this would cause Perla to change her mind in regards to her new found faith. When Perla came to visit us here in Southern California, she didn't ask us to take her to Disneyland, to a fashionable mall or for a scenic drive around Southern California, but I knew the Lord had accomplished his work of redemption in Perla's life when she asked us if we would please take her to Wednesday night prayer meeting. When Perla returned home to the Philippines, the whole Labrador family became sick with the chicken pox. When Perla became ill, instead of the chicken pox growing outward, it went inward, choking off her breath. She was rushed to the hospital emergency, where she was given oxygen, but instead of the oxygen filling her lungs, it blew up her head just like a toy balloon. At that very moment, Perla was in the very presence of Jesus. Perla left behind her wheelchair, leg braces and crutches for a crown of Glory.

CORRUPTIBLE   INCORRUPTIBLE
EARTH?   CROWN.

Mike Lacanilao's sister, Gloria, and I continued our friendship through letter writing. As time went on, Gloria became administrative secretary there at the radio station. Many times when thinking of a missionary, people think only of a "preacher" or someone with a white face, but this isn't always true. A missionary can also be a secretary or one of their own countrymen. Besides working at the radio station there on the Christian Radio City compound, Gloria married and raised two beautiful children. Her son came here to the States to attend Moody Bible Institute of Chicago. I have had to learn although a person might not have grown up as a "handicapped" child, sometimes a person may become "handicapped" later on in life. Sometimes this can become far more difficult than being taught from a very early age how you must accept yourself as a "handicapped" person. I never realized during our stay in the Philippines, my own dear friend, Gloria, would become a case in point. We don't always understand the ways of our Lord; however, it isn't for us to question, only to trust. It was heart rending for me to learn of Gloria becoming blind. Although Gloria is now physically blind, her spiritual eyes continue to see clearly the depth of Christ's love. Gloria is a rich blessing to those who come visit C.R.C.M. CORRUPTIBLE EARTH? INCORRUPTIBLE CROWN.

I knew in fuller reality we were back in the States again when the phone rang one day and it was the Crippled Children's Society of Los Angeles. We hadn't heard from them for years. They didn't even know we had been out of the country.

As the phone call seemed to indicate, we were invited to a Christmas party for all the campers who ever went to Pivika camp. It gave me a feeling of self-confidence knowing I had been able to go back up to camp two or three times without getting homesick. It was profitable for me to learn I could maintain a close bond with my parents and still have an enjoyable time apart from them. The bonding between parent and child is very strong even normally, even more so when the child is handicapped. Very often it's equally as difficult for the parents to let go. I realize since becoming an adult how beneficial it would have been in my earlier years of continuous physical therapy if my parents had some provision on a regular basis for a place of professional care and security for me so they could get away by themselves for a few days or even a short weekend. Grandpa tried to help as much as he could but it wasn't enough to relieve the pressure especially on mother, but she always seemed to have an inward spiritual grace and strength that sustained all three of us through the rough places. Helping parents of handicapped children over the rough places is only one reason why Pivika was such a wonderful place. The Crippled Children's Society of Los Angeles is located on a huge portion of property large enough to accommodate everyone who had ever sang songs around the campfire at Pivika. Pivika had played a part in all of our lives to prepare us for adult living. The most outstanding feature on the program, as I remember it, was Dale Evans Rogers.

She sang, *Somewhere over the Rainbow*. In the middle of her song she gave a public testimony of her personal faith to her living hope in Jesus Christ and eternal life, *Somewhere over the Rainbow*. It was at Pivika camp where one of our counselors read to us, *Angel Unaware*. Through Dale Evans' own sufferings, she had been able to comfort others who suffer. CORRUPTIBLE EARTH? INCORRUPTIBLE CROWN.

The backyard of the Crippled Children's Society was overcrowded. The folding chairs were squeezed in together; the CP girl seated next to me had just graduated from high school. To show how proud she was of her accomplishment she was smoking a cigarette. She was a big girl now and felt herself to be very adult. The only trouble was that she was so severely handicapped she could hardly hold the cigarette between her two fingers. The more she shook, the longer the ashes became. The ashes were just about to fall into my lap. I thought to myself many times, if I ever write a book, I'll never forget this. As handicapped children, we have been taught early that we should try to be as "normal" as possible. However, there seems to be a point of limitation to which we can go without making ourselves appear even more handicapped. This is where our rest in the Lord is so important. This young lady's high school diploma said a bushel for her intellect and maturity. She didn't need to smoke a cigarette.

God grant me the serenity to accept
the things I cannot change,
Courage to change those things I can
and wisdom to know the difference.

By Reinhold Niebuhr

While at the Christmas party, I had the pleasure of seeing Mrs. Adams again, the Principal of Washington Boulevard School. What a very special person. I was really too young to realize just how special Mrs. Adams really was and what a blessing to my mother. Through the years, mother never forgot to talk about Mrs. Adams. We weren't able to talk much with her at the party, but just to see her was for us a serendipity.

I'm sure we have many friends, without our realizing it, who are waiting for us *Somewhere over the Rainbow*, but our memories never leave us. Mrs. Adams called me Diana Blissard. If the name was wrong, certainly she got the association correct. This was amazing to me after not seeing her for all those years and the many different types of handicapped children who had come through her professional life. Diana Blissard, as you will recall, was the Cerebral Palsy girl whom mother was able to help during the time we lived in Inglewood, California. Diana went to Washington Boulevard School and also Pivika camp. To be perfectly honest about it, I wondered how Mrs. Adams could have thought I was Diana. Diana was a Spastic Cerebral Palsy. Her legs and body movements are very stiff and it's a tremendous effort for her to walk. My physical therapist told me I was fortunate to be an Athatoyt Cerebral Palsy instead of Spastic. Although my physical involvement is general, affecting my speech, balance and coordination, I am free of any stiffness. Therefore, it's much easier to be active. I praise the Lord for His mercy, as the injury at birth could have been much more severe. Sometimes I consider myself a capable person, then at other times I remind myself of the girl with the cigarette, having very normal thoughts and ambitions but going far beyond my limitations for my condition. This is sometimes hard to commit to the Lord when my desire to do things are very strong. Sort of like writing this book, which hopefully a few people will read, as not many stories like these have been written. "A false balance is an abomination to the Lord, but a just weight is His delight. Proverbs 11:1

Although I was in my later years as a teenager, my thoughts still weren't as much on the boys as perhaps they should have been for a young lady of my age. While still at the Christmas party, mother saw a CP young man whom she thought was more like me, not too handicapped but just someone who could understand me. Likewise, I would be able to understand and care for him. Even though this was a good intention of my mother, she told me a few years later that I didn't even seem interested. I remind myself of the song that says, *My heart belongs to Daddy because my daddy treats it so well.*

Only a few years ago I did come across the kind of person I would like to marry. He was a Cerebral Palsy person like me, his condition wasn't severe. I met him in a restaurant. He came up to me seemingly wanting to talk while his wife went on to their car almost as if she were willing to let him talk to me. The fact of his already being married just seemed to indicate to me what a nice guy he must have been. I thought to myself, even my cousin Harry who isn't handicapped in anyway would have enjoyed having this regular sort of guy for a friend even though he did walk sort of funny. The badge he wore on his shirt seemed to indicate his place of employment, perhaps some industrial plant. The keys to their car in his hands seemed to tell me he was able to drive. I admired him as much as I could admire anyone. If he would have been able to take care of me, he certainly was the type of fellow I would like to take care of and make a home.

He let me know he was happily married and told me the secret to a happy marriage is not to marry too young. He and his wife were both older when they got married.

His wife wasn't handicapped herself. She married him because he was a very special kind of person. I though if he hadn't already been married, perhaps he could have liked me. He said, "Kay, it's too bad I'm already married." Whether I ever marry or not, isn't important to me. My desire is the directive will of God for my life.

> "For My thoughts are not your thoughts,
> Neither are your ways, My
> ways, declares the Lord.
> For as the heavens are
> higher than the earth,
> So are My ways higher than your ways,
> And My thoughts than your thoughts.
>
> Isaiah 55:8,9

I wouldn't marry a person unless he was a born again Christian. On the other hand, I wouldn't marry a person just because he was a Christian or handicapped. I believe when two people come together in a marriage, they need to be meant for each other in order for there to be a more perfect union. If a person should happen to be handicapped, this would be fine with me.

Thinking back, when leaving the Philippines, it seemed as though we would never see our Filipino friends again this side of our Eternal Home where would be our endless joy of fellowship, where there will be no good-byes. Isn't saying goodbye just another part of what missionary life is all about? It seems as though I've had to say goodbye so many times in my life, why doesn't it become easier?

One day mother found me crying in my bedroom closet. "Kay, why are you crying?" "Look mom,' I said, "look at all my shoes lined up across the floor. Our Filipino ladies don't have any shoes." Because of my being the only child with all personal needs and wants satisfied, I believe it's been profitable for me to see the extreme sufferings in other parts of the world. It's given me lots of peace in the knowledge of my heart being able to be broken concerning some of the things that break God's heart. Each of us have our own pain and sufferings but how blessed it is to be able to cry over the pains and sufferings of someone else. The Lord has been extremely gracious to us as Americans. How long will we continue to receive from His bountiful hand if we willfully persist in breaking His heart because of our sin?

Before we left the Philippines, mother took the foot prints of each one of our Filipino ladies in hopes our family would gradually be able to buy each of the 25 Filipino staff a brand new pair of her very own store bought shoes. The traditional shoe of the Philippines is a wooden platform style with a plastic toe. These are called Bakya. Shoes are very important to every lady. This is why most American women have a closet full of them. One pair for each color scheme and another one just in case it might be useful. This would be the very first pair of shoes our Filipino ladies ever owned.

One day mother was talking to a department store manager about our Filipino believers concerning their special needs for clothing and shoes. The man quickly went to the back of the store, took off his own clothes to give to mother to be sent to the PI. One reason I believe God has blessed

America, is her trust in God and willingness to share with others around the world. Our conservative Baptist church here in Fullerton asked to be given the opportunity to share in sending shoes to the Philippines.

Filipinos just love to come to America. Isaac Atienza, eldest son of Max and Sarah Atienza, after he had been here in the States for several years went to Seattle Pacific College, became an American citizen and married an American girl, graduated from Seattle Pacific and became a public school teacher. He told me once when he came to visit us with his wife, Carole, and their little girl, Michelle, "The Filipinos when they come here to the states they go bananas. I thought to myself, "Ike, you sure ought to know." Ike Atienza is now a very successful man living in the Seattle, Washington, area. The entire Atienza family is now living in Washington State. They are as American as mama's apple pie. One summer, Ike, Carole and little Michelle came to visit us here in Fullerton as they had done many times before. Once Ike put his dark brown arm up next to my arm that had been browned by the sun. We made a very good match. Ike knew already my heart was Filipino, too. The Atienza family as well as most of the Lacanilao family are here in the states, but my dream is to see my dear Gloria Lacanilao Aquarino again.

Once a Filipino friend came to visit us and said, "Kay, don't you have any Filipino neighbors? You really do need some Filipino neighbors." It seems as though she was concerned about my future in the event that I wouldn't have my parents any longer, but if I had some Filipino neighbors, I would certainly be all right.

Soon after returning to the states, I gave a call to Mrs. Brown, our beloved school teacher from Lathrop Junior High School, to let her know I still remembered her and appreciated her years of devotion to the physically handicapped. If ever the Cerebral Palsy Foundation had a champion on their side, it was Mrs. Brown. At the time of my call, Mrs. Brown was very much up in years yet I sensed within her a feeling of discouragement; a feeling that somehow she wasn't needed anymore even though she was very tired and certainly had earned some relaxation alone with her husband. I tried to encourage her the best I knew how but of course I was still very young. I appreciate her now the way I should have appreciated her then. She wanted to know if I would be returning to the special class at Lathrop. I told her I would continue my correspondence school and finish the eighth grade. If I could have stayed at Washington Blvd School, then graduated from the eighth grade, I could have gone to Whitney High School, another fine school for physically handicapped students. This is one of the sacrifices I had to make in following my parents in missionary service. But it seems the Lord made it all up to me in the realization of my being able to travel with my parents to many parts of the Orient and across the United States. This is one of the advantages of being raised in a missionary family. When parents are committed to their missionary calling, the Lord takes care of their children. MK's (missionary kids) receive as much education and knowledge of the world, if not more, than if they stayed in one corner of it.

The Lord was so precious to give me eighteen or nineteen wonderful years in Temple Baptist church. It seems as though all through my life the Lord has always provided something needed just at the right time. Temple Baptist Church played a very important part in establishing my life in the Word of God. I can never think of Temple Church without thinking of Harry Pulver, our high school Sunday school teacher, and later on, our college age young peoples' sponsor. Harry was special because he was a completed Jew. Harry told us once he liked the idea of salvation by grace because this means you can get something for nothing. It's a good deal. Harry didn't have much more than a grammar school education. However, just as the rest of the high school and then college people would say about Harry, "If Harry didn't know the answer to something, he would always try to find it." Harry was a real student of the Bible. Just like Mrs. Brown, Harry, too, wanted us to be the very best we could, young people and future adults for the Lord. The Lord even had a future for Harry, as he became the Chaplain for the Orange County prison ministries. Harry continued to be diligent in the study of God's word until one day he was called to be the pastor of the community church in San Pasqual near Escondido. Just before Harry went to be with the Lord, Billy Graham would always make a special effort to visit Harry's church. Harry, as I knew him, was very high strung, never still it seemed but his every move was for the Lord. CORRUPTIBLE EARTH? INCORRUPTIBLE CROWN.

I think my friend Harry forgot to tell the high school young people our salvation wasn't really a free gift. It cost our precious Savior the ultimate price of Calvary. It was a good deal for us but for Him it cost everything. The part

I like the best is the empty tomb. Our precious Lord will never need to die again; because He lives, we also shall never die.

One day Harry told the young people a little more of his Christian testimony. He told us of how his family completely disowned him after he accepted Christ as his Jewish Messiah. They even had a burial service for him just as if he were dead. There are some types of sufferings that go far beyond that of physical affliction. Religious persecution has been felt around the world. We don't like to think of it being here in America, the land of freedom, but it is certainly here.

CORRUPTIBLE EARTH?   INCORRUPTIBLE CROWN.

Woody and Jewel Hudson, pastors of Temple Baptist Church, also played a very important part in my spiritual growth just as Harry Pulver. They built Temple Church from just a handful of people to almost eleven hundred members. For a time while the church was still very small, we were very much like an intimate family. It was a sorrowful time for all of us when the Hudson's decided to leave the church. They had nourished the church through its years of infancy during the toddler years and had brought the church up to maturity. For a short time we felt, as a body of believers, as if we were left without spiritual parents. The Hudson's had accepted an opportunity offered to them by the Conservative Baptist board of missions. Their new position would take them traveling around the world. Woody's original vision for the church had only half materialized. The sanctuary and day school were still in the future. One evening after a young peoples social, I happened to be riding in the car with the interim pastor of the congregation, Pastor Chase Sawtell of Biola. Everything in the car was quiet for a time. I certainly didn't know what to say. I just felt privileged that the pastor would be assigned to take me home. Pastor Sawtell was the one to break the silence. "Kay," he said, "I really do envy you." I thought to myself, 'now why would a preacher of the gospel ever envy me.' He continued talking, "Envy you, Kay, because you have lots of time for study." I knew I was perfectly safe riding with the pastor but, to be honest about it, I kind of wondered what he was driving at besides driving the car. "Kay," he continued, "I would like to buy you a correspondence Bible course from Moody Bible Institute in Chicago. I thought to myself: 'Well, Lord, you've always supplied my every need, now you are doing it again.' I've often thought if the Lord had allowed things to be different than they were and I hadn't had the injury from birth, I would have gone to Moody Bible Institute. I'd heard they have an excellent course on foreign missions.

ADDED BLESSINGS

Traveling across America with my parents gave me much more understanding for the teenager in Manilla who asked me, "Why is it, Kay, we have to be out here in the Philippines when we have a beautiful country of our own?" It was truly breathtaking, at times, as we traveled through many of our National State Parks such as Zion National Park in all of its majestic wonderment. It seemed as if we were driving through a national cathedral carved out of rock. Aspen National Park was of special interest to me. I fell in love with the white bark Poplar trees and the beaver, diligent at his work building his dams. A true entrepreneur if ever there was one. It seems to me if the beaver were able to talk, he would say to handicapped people everywhere, "We all have our disabilities in one way or another. If I can make it, so can you." Traveling through middle America, the great plane states, I almost felt the desire to wave back at those amber waves of grain. I found myself enraptured by the fields upon fields of corn in the state of Iowa, the corn state, where, "*the corn is as high as an elephants eye and it looks like its climbing clear up to the sky.*" *O WHAT A BEAUTIFUL MORNING.* All this caused us to realize how fortunate we were to be actually viewing with our own eyes the same scenic treasure which inspired Kathy Lee Bates to write, *AMERICA THE BEAUTIFUL.* However, there was a far more significant purpose in our lonely odyssey across the open planes in a fifteen foot trailer which was being pulled behind our car. As returned missionaries, my parents had first hand knowledge of field operations which would be of interest to individuals and churches who consider the Far East Broadcasting Co. their prayer and financial giving mission project. Also, our purpose was to acquaint other churches that hadn't heard about the F.E.B.C. ministry before.

Looking back, it seems my most memorable days of our deputation trips across the country was our three months stay at Winona Lake, Indiana. It seems as though I've already shared much earlier in this writing some personal feelings concerning the Youth for Christ International conference. This youth convention was really the highlight of the whole conference season. During the Youth for Christ extravaganza, it seems I recall meeting a very special young lady in the lounge of the Winona Lake Hotel. She was the Winona Lake representative of Moody Science films. I remember her most of all for her deep spiritual insight. Joan, as I'll choose to call her, not being sure of having the right name after so many years gone by, was an inspiration to everyone, especially her husband. Joan had the ability to fill every cloudy day with sunshine. She certainly did so for me. Words like, 'I can't,' just didn't seem to be in Joan's vocabulary. She reminded me of the beaver up the creek in Aspen National Park, because of her determination. It just so happened that Joan had been born without her left arm. Joan told me, "I tried to wear an artificial arm, but hated it. It made me feel handicapped." Just living at Winona Lakes was quite an experience for me as I remember it.

Fortunately we had wonderful Christian neighbors with whom to leave our home in responsible care. At times, I personally had the privilege of staying in their home when my parents would be gone on short deputation trips for the radio ministry. The Drakes always made me feel a part of their family; we appreciated them so very much. We were able to see the provision of the Lord for our needs in the most tangible way, and His timing was always perfect far beyond our own comprehension.

Winona Lake, Indiana, as well as being a Bible conference grounds with the Billy Sunday Tabernacle was, also, the home of the Grace Brethren College and Seminary. The Lord's provision was again made available for us, as students were away on summer vacation and a mobile home was left in excellent condition for our use.

I'm sure I'll long remember our very unusual next door neighbors. They were a young married couple studying for the gospel ministry. Both of them had grown up on the farm; they had never experienced city life before. Winona Lake was situated between Indianapolis and Warsaw, two metropolitan cities. One day our neighbors brought home a raccoon on their return trip from the country. They cared for him as if they were his parents. Since they didn't have any children, the raccoon became the center of their affection. One day while our neighbors were gone on a short shopping trip, the raccoon was left in full charge of the trailer. He took control of the situation as only a raccoon would know how. When his 'parents' got home, they opened the door of their humble home to the biggest surprise of their lives. The raccoon had remained true to his natural instincts and, of course, everything was on the floor including the flour and sugar bins. The cupboards were emptied, as well. Just as most parents, the young couple seemed to think their baby was cute. If I am ever inclined to forget anything about Winona Lake, it certainly won't be, Joshua, the raccoon.

Indianapolis is the city I enjoyed most of all. Warsaw, in my opinion, wasn't much to write home about. During free time from correspondence school, I was able to help mother and dad in the Far East Broadcasting Company store. This is where we set up displays of all different kinds to interest people in missions. A twenty-four hour, seven day a week challenge for us, to be perfectly honest about it. We were able to catch most all the people going and coming from the Billy Sunday Tabernacle across the street. One of the few times we were able to get away for the day we went north to Chicago.

We hadn't been back to Chicago since I was a toddler, not yet able to walk on my own. It was at the Cook County Hospital in Chicago where my parents first learned of my Cerebral Palsy diagnosis. My parents were able to show me the very house where we had lived in a small upstairs apartment. Our landlady happened to be working at the Cook County Hospital, one of the finest hospitals in the nation at that time. She said to my mother one day, "You know, Margaret, your little daughter reminds me of those children I see everyday at the hospital." This was the beginning process of my rehabilitation. The visiting nurses association was sent out to train mother to give me physical therapy.

As a strong, healthy 18-year-old teenager, visiting Chicago once again was almost like returning to my roots. It was very important for me to reflect back upon the goodness of the Lord for giving me parents who would not only follow doctors, but also the guidance of the Holy Spirit. To any child, this is a treasure.

When returning home, having my correspondence school completed, it was time to turn our thoughts toward the future. I'm so thankful for having parents who gave me lots of encouragement while at the same time being careful not to build air castles which would some day crumble at my feet. If you can't do great things, do small things great. My parents were also diligent not only in physical rehabilitation but likewise in my psychological and emotional development, which is a continual process.

AND GOD SAID, "NO"

I asked God to make my handicapped
child whole, and God said, "No."
He said her spirit is whole, her
body is only temporary.

By Claudia Minden Welsz

My parents, as well as myself, were concerned that it was time for thinking about finding something I could do at home to keep my mind occupied as well as giving my hands therapy and improving my coordination. We wondered if having a weaving loom would be the answer as this is something I was taught in school. We got in touch with the rehabilitation center in Santa Ana, not realizing in doing so, this would be another turning point, confronting an even truer evaluation of myself and recommitment to the will of God.

It was at this time in my development that I had to make an even greater surrender of my life to the Sovereignty of God and control of the Holy Spirit. This was difficult for a very ambitious person in my condition. For this reason the Lord has had to deal harshly with me at times. Reality never fits our dreams. What God plans for us is far better than even our dreams. He has shown me if I had been all wrapped up in my own professional life, I would have absolutely no time for Him. "For I know the plans that I have for you," declares the Lord, "plans for welfare and not calamity to give you a future and a hope." Jeremiah 29:11

What hope would any of us have if this present world were the only life? We who believe in the resurrection of the dead would be the ones most miserable if it were not true.

The rehabilitation center in Santa Ana referred us to the United Cerebral Palsy Foundation of Los Angeles for evaluation with hope of possible job placement. It was a relief to be sent to UCP. I'm always more at ease with folks I feel understand my condition and appreciate me for the person I am. It seems as though I always make a very good first impression and give the appearance of being more capable than I am. This can be as frustrating and disappointing to those who work with me as it is to me. This, too, is something I've had to cast upon the Lord.

Looking back on this portion of my life, I see it as the most humbling of my experiences to find out my true self, yet it was a part of my life I wouldn't trade for any other. I keep telling myself we will understand so many things in eternity that we don't really need to understand right now. Our only need at the moment is to trust. This is sometimes difficult for a person like me who would like to have all the answers right now. It has been excruciatingly painful for me at times to be almost normal yet not able to compete. Through the years, however, I have discovered others who are in a similar or the same situation. Hopefully this testimony can reassure them they aren't alone.

During our first interview with the administrative office of the foundation, they were interested in knowing something of my background and the reason for my becoming a CP person. At this time, I was asked to leave the room and the interview proceeded with my parents retelling the story of how I happened to be born in Danzig. As my parents are able to relay it, being born in the city of Danzig, in 1939, wasn't exactly the best of times. My parents have told many times of living out of suitcases during the invasion of Hitler's storm troopers into nearby countries and Hitler's personal control over the minds and hearts of much of the German people. The persecution of the Jewish people was displayed in every store window. American friendship toward Israel wasn't appreciated. To be an American during this time of German history wasn't exactly to find favor. My parents knew the Lord had called them to a very needful work. The mission where they were serving had been operating an orphanage, a Bible institute and church. Dad was in control of all administration operations. All during mother's pregnancy, my parents were knowledgeable of the threat of impending war.

It was needful for my parents to keep in continual readiness in the event it would be necessary to flee for their lives. It was in the midst of this mounting tension that mother was about to deliver. Dad had been sent to a hospital across the city to have an emergency surgery on his spine. He had already been bed ridden for weeks. Simultaneously, mother was in another hospital at the other end of the city. At the conclusion of four days and five nights, mother had a raging fever and was at deaths door.

My dad had no knowledge whatsoever of the suffering going on at the opposite end of the city. Dad told us, as I was growing up, if he had known the truth of what was going on, he could have demanded a Caesarian section be performed. Although a surgery of this nature was against German practice, we could have demanded our rights as free Americans.

My parents had been first hand witnesses of much of the persecuted church in Eastern Europe and considered it an honor to have been even a small part of it. Many of the Bible School students had been beaten and left for dead along the roadside for preaching the gospel of Christ. Some were imprisoned many times and beaten. After being released they would go back to preach again. We feel what we have given for the gospel is so very small compared with those who have given their blood.

After four days and five nights, mother in her state of delirium in the cold basement of a German hospital, had to plead with the doctor in the German language to please take her child. We don't like to accuse the doctor of any wrong doing, although he was a Nazi Black Shirt, but I do personally believe they could have done much more to make mother more comfortable. It just doesn't seem right that they waited so long or didn't really care to alleviate mother's prolonged suffering. When the doctor went inside mother with his instruments to pull me out, my head snapped back causing injury to three areas of the cerebellum, causing what my parents were to learn later to be Cerebral Palsy.

After the private interview between my parents and counselor they came into the waiting area where I was seated. The counselor reassured me she knew I could have told this story to her just as well as my parents, but it was the foundations policy to only discuss such things with parents. I appreciated her show of confidence in my intelligence.

The very next day we were scheduled for a visit with the doctor. Much to our surprise, it was Dr. Jones. We hadn't seen her since my days at Children's Hospital. There seemed to be no time to talk about the intervening years that had flown by so quickly. Certainly, Dr. Jones had no knowledge of my academic achievement because of being given the electric typewriter or of our experience in the Philippines. Certainly our knowledge of Dr. Jones had been limited to the therapy department of Children's Hospital. In just a few years, Dr. Jones had risen to be one of the most outstanding orthopedic surgeons in the entire United States and had been the private doctor of President Kennedy's parents.

Dr. Jones gave me an evaluation test of my Cerebral Palsy condition in front of a panel of student doctors. At the end of the procedure, my CP was classified as mild. As most often human nature tries to take all the credit to one's self, with the right intentions to be sure, Dr. Jones tried to give most of the credit to mother and I. Mother, who could have taken much more of the praise herself, was able to give testimony to our Great Physician. It was delightful to see the smiles on one or two of the faces on the panel of student doctors. It took courage for them to show their pleasure in what mother had to say. It took even more courage for mother to say what she did. We never know the lives we will touch when we allow the blessed Holy Spirit to use us as a witness for our Lord.

After a full week of testing both mental and manual dexterity, it was determined that although I had a knowledge of how to do things, there was a tremor in my hands which wouldn't allow my work production to be able to earn minimum wage. The tremor became more severe as I would try to work faster.

At this point, once again, I couldn't help thinking of the girl with the cigarette who I criticized in my heart at the summer camp Christmas party. I was hoping to qualify for a normal employment. At the UCP Foundation, I was once again confronted with real truth about myself. I realize as I look back on it now the Lord was working with me in the area of my selfish pride. If Christ isn't Lord of every area of our lives, He isn't our Lord at all. I have had to renew this commitment of my life to the Lord many times.

At the conclusion of all evaluations, it was decided to be necessary for me to work in a shelter area. My counselor told me I could do anything I wanted to do in life if I had all the time in the world to do it. I didn't know whether to take this as a compliment or an insult. The thought was expressed of my possible need to be more involved with people. I love to share with others. Perhaps this comes from our experience in the PI.

I was greatly relieved to have the week of testing over not realizing new experiences of self-evaluation lay just ahead. The UCP Foundation of Los Angeles sent me to Goodwill Industries of Santa Ana. This is where my system had the shock of its life.

As a general rule, most teenagers have been prepared for the workaday world by helping their mothers and taking responsibilities at home. This wasn't required of me. Coming home from school each evening, I would be completely exhausted. It was all I could do just to get my homework finished in order to keep up even partially with Mrs. Peterson's class of normal students and get ready for the next day. At Goodwill Industries, all at once, I was being called upon to be dynamite or at least to my point of view.

It was a privilege for me to be accepted by Goodwill as very few Cerebral Palsy persons are chosen. I'm thankful now for my experience at Goodwill because I can better understand others who punch a time clock for eight hours, five days a week.

My parents provided my transportation each day. I clocked in every morning at 7:30, and clocked out at 4:30 in the afternoon. First thing each morning was chapel service. I learned that a Methodist minister started the Goodwill.

One day my dad was asked to give the morning devotional. He talked about, "Moses' Rod." "What is that in your hand?" With the thought in mind if all we have in our hand is just an ordinary rod, if we give it to the Lord, He will use it. This I felt was an excellent message for the employees of Goodwill.

Once while sitting in Chapel with a friend, I mentioned to her how wonderful it seemed that Goodwill was Christian. She just laughed at me. "Kay," she said, "if you think everyone at Goodwill is a Christian, you just have to be very naïve." She proceeded to tell me about the woman who was found walking out the door with three dresses underneath her own dress. Some of the employees at Goodwill Industries are what is called, "socially handicapped". Some of them have a prison record and wouldn't be able to get work any place else except Goodwill.

One of the employees in the construction department where I worked told a joke about the doughnut and the cake. The doughnut said to the cake, "If I had all the dough you've got, I wouldn't be hanging around this hole." Just as my dad had the perfect sermon for Goodwill, this one employee certainly had the perfect joke. One CP man of middle age working at Goodwill was in his younger years a nuclear scientist with the Atomic Energy Commission. When at last he realized they were using his brilliance to make bombs to kill people, he had a complete nervous breakdown from which he never fully recovered. It was at Goodwill where he has been able to rebuild a new life.

Here at Goodwill I was given the job of folding the Goodwill bags. I was told that because of the tremor and coordination problem, I didn't qualify for a better job. They even discussed the possibility of my living independently but decided I would always need someone to do my cooking. Whenever I'm told I can't do something, that's the very thing I want to do or at least try it. At Goodwill I got to where I was able to complete four sacks of bags in eight hours. There were about 250 bags in each sack. I was taught the method of folding several bags at one time. I was able to manage two sacks in the morning and two in the afternoon. By the time I arrived home in the evening, I was exhausted. I hadn't worked that hard in all my life. Not even for my mother. The complete exhaustion and tension built up during the day made it impossible to sleep at night. The head boss of our department kept telling me they gave me the easiest job in the whole place, just as if I didn't know it. Raymond, I told his story earlier in this writing, was working in the same department. Ray had progressed to where he was able to go back to the Fullerton school system. He was a high school graduate. Fortunately, Ray's coordination was quite good and he was able to complete about ten to twelve sacks a day that provided for some sort of independent living. Sometimes it was difficult for me to watch other CP persons able to accomplish things I wasn't able to do. Not that I begrudge them the ability to do it, but I felt if they can accomplish all the things they do under their kind of pressure, then why shouldn't I be able to do it, too.

Most often it was easier to see so-called "normal" people perform accomplishments beyond my reach. This seemed to be a matter of fact to be accepted long ago, but to see other physically handicapped, even in wheelchairs, able to accomplish things which were out of bounds for me, I found I had to face it, sometimes with bewilderment, but always with a sense of admiration. There also came a time I had to realize other handicapped individuals were looking back again at me the same way.

It got to the point where I just wasn't able to cope with an eight-hour workday because of the inability to sleep at night. I would clock in at 7:30 in the morning feeling like I should be clocking out because of the complete exhaustion I could feel building up. I felt I was a failure, but the friends I had made during my stay at Goodwill were an encouragement to me. I knew the Lord had a purpose in my being there even though at the time, it was almost impossible to understand the reason why.

It's almost laughable as I look back on the situation now. I can still recall my dad's admonishment to me one evening as I sat in a puddle of my own tears. "Kay, don't you quit, let them fire you, but don't you quit." I thought perhaps my dad understood something I certainly didn't.

The very next morning while sitting in chapel a well-dressed young lady from the front office came up to me. Her legs and body were very short; she reminded me of my friend, Johnny, when we lived in North Hollywood. She was a dwarf but didn't have all the physical deformities that Johnny had. As I was sitting down, she still had to look up to me. As she stretched even further, she whispered in my ear, "Are you a Christian?" I looked at her in consternation while at the same time asking the Lord, "Why?" I was so discouraged at this point, I didn't even feel like a Christian. She, likewise, told me of her love for the Lord and we had wonderful fellowship.

I was thankful for Christian fellowship and the chapel services each morning, as I wasn't taking any time out for private devotions at home. It got to the point where I wasn't able to cope with a full eight-hour day. This posed a great embarrassment to me. How could I get off so easy, working only four hours when everyone else had to work eight? I was certain I would be misunderstood, written off as a lazy person, but I didn't know what else to do about it. This would pose a double hardship on my parents. Up until now my dad was providing all my transportation each morning to the South side of Santa Ana before driving to his place of work in Whittier. Mrs. Blackwell, the top boss over our construction department, had to notify the State government as Goodwill was being paid for keeping me as a "trainee." I wasn't being paid anything. I discovered working half day was something I could handle, although working at Goodwill wouldn't provide me with any sort of independent living. The only money I saw while working at Goodwill was the dime I found in the women's restroom. I thought I was smart to buy myself a milk. I realize now I should have kept the dime for posterity. I happened to mention once to Mrs. Blackwell that I would like to write a book someday. At this point, I never really though I would, I just wanted to use Mrs. Blackwell as a sounding board to see what she would say. I told her I didn't think I'd be able to do so because I had no education. She said, "Kay, it doesn't matter at all. You can still write a book." I was astonished at her display of confidence in me. She continued talking, "Kay," she said, "the only reason for your not being able to work here at Goodwill would be transportation. I was waiting for them to fire me. Perhaps deep down in their hearts they were wishing they could.

One afternoon, just before my "trainee" program was to come to a conclusion, one of the administration executives from the front office brought a group of businessmen on a tour of the Goodwill plant. When he came around to my station, he told the visitors, "Now this girl has the will to work, but not the coordination." One of the white-collar professional men bent down to my ear and said, "I'd rather have the will." This encouragement meant so much to me, as I had been so discouraged. I even felt I had been a failure.

As I recall my days at Goodwill Industries, it seems I had a few girl friends but not a great deal. It was the boys who gave me the most trouble. I can still remember our school teacher, Mrs. Brown, telling me one day, "Kay, if you hadn't been handicapped, your parents would have had very serious trouble with the boys," almost as if my parents were fortunate that I was handicapped. I never fully understood what Mrs. Brown was talking about until I came here to Goodwill. I had never had a fella flirt with me before.

Besides, throwing me kisses across the room, to my point of view, seemed to be a crude way of going about it. I can remember thinking, 'these guys sure must be hard up for a woman, they don't even care if she's handicapped.' Most of the gals on the outside of these walls wouldn't even give these guys a second look. Although I couldn't feel much flattered by their attention, my heart went out to these men. They had no one to really care.

I never consider myself a single person because I'm part of the bride of Christ. Our bridegroom is coming for us soon. We will see him face-to-face. As a hymn says,

> I'm in love, deeply in love,
> His love has made me whole,
> I'm in love with Jesus.

> By Aaron David

My one and only true passion is for Him.

As my parents are approaching their twilight years, they have told me if they had their lives to live over again, they would still serve the Lord. Thirty-five years with the Far East Broadcasting Co., forty-seven in mission work all together. It's really hard to believe we've been home for thirty-two years from the Philippines.

> "I have been young and now I'm old:
> Yet I have not seen the righteous forsaken,
> Or his descendents begging bread."

> Psalms 37:35

None of us can know what the future holds, it isn't for us to know, but one thing is for certain to us who are members of God's forever family. CORRUPTIBLE EARTH? INCORRUPTIBLE CROWN.

The End

Katherine L. Bronson

ABOUT THE AUTHOR

Discover firsthand from Kay, the cerebral palsy daughter of missionary parents who began their missionary life in the Russian and Eastern European Mission, then became members of the original staff at the Far East Broadcasting Company (FEBC).

CPSIA information can be obtained
at www.ICGtesting.com
Printed in the USA
FSOW04n2213061015
11897FS

9 781512 707564